In God's Hands

Broken NOT Shattered

A Memoir of Hope

MARY MARKHAM

In God's Hands
Broken NOT Shattered-A Memoir of Hope

Author: Mary Markham
Editors: Marla McKenna, Lyda Rose Haerle
Associate Editor: Griffin Mill
Cover Design: Gillian E. Miller
Interior Layout: Michael Nicloy

In God's Hands

Broken NOT Shattered
A Memoir of Hope

ISBN: 978-1945907425

Published by Nico 11 Publishing & Design
Quantity order requests can be emailed to:
mike@nico11publishing.com

N11

Be well read.

I dedicate this book to my mom who passed away from pancreatic cancer. She always encouraged me to never give up and believed I would one day write a book.

To my loving husband Craig, a gift from God 30,000 feet in the air. You have been my rock and gentle giant since the day I met you! Thank you for your unconditional love, support, and encouragement to write this book.

To my beautiful children, Michelle and Nik, my precious gifts from God. Thank you for your unending love, support, encouragement, gentle reminders to take my own advice, and of course, adding your wonderful sense of humor when I need it the most.

And to my amazing stepsons, Mitchell and Austin, who complete this beautiful unconditional loving blended family!

I love you all!

TABLE OF CONTENTS

Hope IS IN THE HEART OF THE BELIEVER

FOREWORD

Life has often been described as a journey with ups and downs, unexpected turns, roadblocks, and detours. Along the journey we encounter people who love and support us, guide and encourage us, but also, unfortunately, others who discourage us and wound us and damage us. Our personal histories of the journey often contain sorrow, pain, disappointment and betrayal as well as joy, love, healing and friendship. As a Pastor for the past forty years, I have been privileged to share in the journey of many people, one of whom is the author of this book, Mary Markham. Her journey is one of moving from darkness and negativity to light and hopefulness.

As you will discover in reading this book, Mary faced many negative experiences on her journey, often from the very people she loved and trusted. She shares honestly about dealing with her parents' divorce, her sexual abuse by a family member, her troubled marriage, her miscarriages, the difficult birth of her son, her divorce, her loneliness and fears.

I have been part of this journey with Mary for over twenty-five years. We met in a NICU hospital room in Jackson, Michigan, where I baptized her newborn son Nik. Nik was born premature, and Mary was told he wouldn't make it through the night. I then sat with Mary, holding her hand as we cried and prayed together for him, and the staff prepared to transfer him by helicopter to Children's Hospital in Ann Arbor. Unbeknownst to me at the time, our prayers were answered and Nik did not need to go to Ann Arbor after all. Through the skills of the doctors and nurses at the hospital in Jackson, Nik pulled through and is a happy, healthy adult today! In this experience with Mary, I discovered her genuine faith and trust in God. Her prayer that night and in so many other difficult situations is "to Let Go and Let God," that is, to place everything in the hands of God, trusting that He will take care of us. "Let God be God" and provide all we need in the present situation is her prayer of confidence. As the years progressed, I noticed that Mary, unlike many other people facing difficulties, discovered the importance of shifting the focus away from herself and her problems, to helping others in their needs. Within our Church community, and then wherever she has lived, Mary has volunteered her time to minister to others and to mentor others. In doing so, she was not always focused on her own needs and wants and pains, but rather on how she could help others carry their burdens. The more she helped others, the more confident she became and the more comfortable she became with herself and her leadership abilities. She grew in compassion and creative ways to share that compassion with others in need. Her ministry to others helped her find a new peacefulness and joy within herself.

Along her journey, Mary recognized the need to surround herself with positive, encouraging and supportive people. She often refers to them as her angels. They help to counterbalance the negative voices that are so common in our lives, the voices that tell us that we're not good enough or smart enough or pretty enough or holy enough. These voices can often fill us with doubt and fear, and hold us back from reaching our full potential. Mary had to break free of these negative people in her life and instead, surround herself with positive friends who truly support and encourage her. As you will read in this book, this decision has allowed her to grow into her true happy self.

Mary and I have remained close spiritual friends over these twenty-five plus years as she moved from Michigan to Arizona to Colorado to Wisconsin. Her faith continues to guide and direct her life. Her passion for serving others has only grown stronger over the years. This book is certainly part of her ministry of service. She shares her story, her journey, with the hope that it may help you on your journey. I hope and pray that, as you read it, you too may come to deepen your trust in the God who loves you, in your desire to share his love with others and that you will surround yourself with loving, positive, supportive friends who challenge you to be your best self!

Rev. John A. Kettelberger, CM
Provincial Director of the Daughters of Charity
St. Louis, Missouri

IN
GOD'S
HANDS

PROLOGUE

There is a time for everything, and a season
for every activity under the heavens.
Ecclesiastes 3:1

AN INSPIRING, RELATABLE, AND HEALING JOURNEY OF HOW FAITH IS DISCERNED A LIFE IN GOD'S HANDS

"WOW! You should write a book!" I was told again after someone heard another one of my life experiences and how I overcame my struggles. For years I thought about writing a book, and on April 18, which just so happened to be the day of my mother's birth, my journal entry began in 2015, "I want to write a book to help others through their struggles we face daily. I want to be able to use my God-given talents to make a difference…it's not easy, but it can be refreshing to know you're not alone." I believe everything happens for a reason, and this book is no different. Its timing was God's timing. He chose the path I took, and He chose the people who came into my life, and the life lessons learned along the way. I never gave up hope, even when I easily could have; I persevered and turned my messes into messages and my trials into triumphs. I chose to walk by faith, not by sight, and I put everything in God's hands.

WHY SEVEN CHAPTERS?

Seven was the number given to me when I prayed about writing this book. When I questioned, *Seven what?* nothing came to me. It was all in God's timing, and I needed patience. During my prayer time, the Holy Spirit's message was clear; seven is the most significant number in the Bible and is considered to be a holy number because in Genesis, "God rested on the 7th day." These seven chapters represent the "Seven gifts of the Holy Spirit."

Life's Journey—Whether it's my life or yours, we all have a journey, a path to follow. We are guided by the Holy Spirit; we hear the still small voice when we listen. We are given "free will" to choose our path or the direction we will follow. At times our choices do not seem the wisest, but I have found we are either learning from them or teaching others through them. We all have gifts. Which gift gives you strength?

1. Fortitude
2. Understanding
3. Fear of the Lord
4. Wisdom
5. Counsel
6. Piety
7. Knowledge

Life is like a good book. At times we may head in one direction, be drawn towards a journey that reflects our own life, or choose one completely opposite in hopes of clearing our cluttered minds. Either way, our life's journey is birthed with a beginning. Each chapter is a gift, and each page we turn or road we take builds us up, teaching us life lessons, giving us purpose and direction for God's plan until we reach the end of our book; our own journey ends but it's not our final destination. How will the last chapter of your journey end?

You are indeed my rock and my fortress for your name's sake lead me and guide me. -Psalm 31:3

I believe everything happens for a reason in the right season. I often wondered why so many things happened in my life the way they did? I believe life doesn't always go the way we want. God had a plan, gave me choices, and when things got tough, I had to put it, whatever "it" was, in God's hands in order to grow deeper personally, spiritually, mentally, and emotionally. I learned how God turned my messes into messages, and my brokenness into a breakthrough.

God put angels in my life, along my journey, to help me stay on the right path. He inspired me to help others as others helped me.

Every time I began to question, worry, or try to figure things out on my own, I struggled. I had to return my focus to God and put whatever good or bad was going on in my life, in His hands. Only then did I realize how something good or great could come out of each situation. I learned how to accept my wounds as layers, peeled away one at a time, to reach the real, raw, and authentic treasure God created me to be.

Although this journey travels from my childhood through marriage, miscarriages, births, divorce, blended families, mentoring, volunteering, growing in my faith, and blessed tenfold, I believe God has a message, something relatable, for each person's own journey. Embrace the message God reveals to you as you turn the pages of my journey; a journey where I have experienced growth in freedom, growth in faith, and growth in hope and charity.

Come along…it's a journey of hope for you too.

CHAPTER ONE

FORTITUDE

Standing up for what is right in the sight of God

A Journey Inspired by an Angel

Be strong and courageous. Do not be afraid or terrified because of them, for the LORD your God goes with you; He will never leave you nor forsake you.

Deuteronomy 31:6 NIV

IMAGINE WHAT LIFE WOULD BE LIKE
IF YOU NEVER TRUSTED GOD

I can only imagine what my life would have been like if I had never heard that still small voice or trusted God.

Are you listening? Trusting?

Mesmerized, I watched and stared out my bedroom window, listening to the music coming from my 45 RPM turntable record player, at the people either entering or leaving the public parking lot. I had just returned from Camp LuWiSoMo, the Christian camp my parents sent me to the summer before fifth grade. (It was a week-long experience of building friendships, developing skills and knowledge to use for the rest of my life through activities that included archery, swimming, canoeing, fishing, hiking, camping, nature skills, arts and crafts, horseback riding, orienteering, team-building, crazy fun games, and even some free time! Each day included faith building experiences, devotions, interactive worship, and ended with a devotion and singing around the campfire.)

I left camp as a different person on the inside, looking at life in a deeper way and appreciating the opportunity to meet a diverse group of kids, some who lived in small towns, and some in big cities and travelled from all over; I couldn't help but wonder where these people in the parking lot came from? How far did they travel? Where were they headed? What were their lives like? What was their story?

I remembered living in the big, green house, next to the public parking lot on the north side of Milwaukee, walking distance to "Bill the Butcher" and "Grebe's Bakery" (where my mom worked while I slept). I attended a parochial elementary school; we had daily dinner prayers before Mom's home cooked meals; and Sunday church services together as a family was normal for us. At church, our family sat towards the front, took up most of the pew, and always dressed in our Sunday best. I loved getting dressed up on Sundays, especially when I wore my black patent leather shoes with my favorite dress. It was the red one with white square patterns and three red decorative buttons centered in the middle of a white laced collar. My favorite part was how pretty I felt when the dressed flared out as I spun around. My life always revolved around my family. The big, green house was a huge duplex, and my grandparents lived upstairs. My grandma was the most selfless person I knew. She and my grandpa were twelve years apart. At times, when I went upstairs to visit, I found her in the bathroom washing Grandpa's face.

"Sit down on the side of the tub if you want, Honey," Grandma would say while she finished shaving and combing his hair.

Few words were said between them, but the love they felt for each other was obvious. Grandpa always looked happy and peaceful, and Grandma wore a gentle, loving smile while she cleaned him up. It was as though she took pride in her act of kindness. It was the kind of unconditional love I hoped to have one day. After my grandpa went to live in the nursing home, my grandma and I shared a room. Our family did everything together including: dinners, prayers, vacations, games, block parties, and everyone was welcome. God created us as one family, so, everyone was accepted, related or not. No judgment or treating anyone differently was allowed. At least this was my perception of our family life.

It felt like we were constantly celebrating something, even friendships. Then without any explanation, because back in the 1970s kids were seen not heard, nor told anything, the celebrations came to a halt, block parties ended, and we moved out of the inner city. It was the beginning of more changes—more than I could have ever imagined. That move eventually, turned into another and another; from the inner city, to the city, and then to the suburbs. This was too far from the life I was accustomed to, but I never dared to ask questions. If I needed to know, I would have been told.

It was like a duplex, but sideways. Our family lived on one side of the townhome and an unknown family resided on the other. By this time my grandpa had passed away, and my grandma wanted to stay in the city, closer to her friends, and an area she was familiar with. It didn't take long for the suburbs to feel more like home in my new environment and with my new friends. Things started to feel good.

IT WAS THE BEST DAY OF MY LIFE!

I wasn't first but I never imagined winning second place in the high jump at the track meet. Although everything was still new to me, while still adjusting to the small-town changes, new school, and new chapter of my life, I began to feel invincible. I no longer feared being the newbie at the middle school. I celebrated the victory with my new friends.

One shouted, "JUST WAIT, TOMORROW THE ENTIRE SCHOOL WILL KNOW YOU WON 2ND PLACE!"

"How's that?" I asked.

"They make a big deal and celebrate the winners on the morning announcements!" my friend said.

Why did that statement make me instantly feel sick to my stomach? I was just having fun, doing something I enjoyed. It wasn't about the recognition or attention. The only attention I really wished for, was my family to be at my track meet cheering me on.

Nonetheless, I was excited about how well I did. I accomplished something I never thought I could do. I was so excited that I didn't even realize I was skipping down the road, singing, and I couldn't wait to share my big news with my family.

I heard a voice from the distance, "MARY!!"

I looked up and my youngest brother was riding his bike as fast as he could towards me.

"Get on! We need to go!" he shouted.

"Go where?" I asked. "I just finished my best ever in the high jump!"

"I'm sorry, but Mom left!" he yelled.

"What do you mean left? Left where?" I asked.

Everything seemed to come to a dead stop. My life, my family, and my excitement; and it was never to be shared, heard at school, or talked about again.

This new chapter in my life turned into one of my darkest nightmares. I knew my parents had marital problems, but at fourteen, I only knew what I knew and didn't understand the rest. My life moved forward and much faster than I ever wanted or could have imagined. The moving truck was there the next day. I thought living in the suburbs was far enough away from the city, now I had to go live in the middle of nowhere. At least it seemed like that to me. Although still in Wisconsin, it was too far from everything I was accustomed to. So, to me, it WAS in the middle of nowhere! The town was so small; it was even unincorporated. This skinny, little, freckle-faced, brunette was even more confused. At this point, I no longer got excited about getting involved in anything or joining a club or sports. No one would come to watch anyway; it'd be too far to drive, or they would be gone before the excitement could set in. I just wanted to be left alone.

Why must I stay with extended family members?

Why can't I just have my mom, dad, and my family life back?

I became quiet, reserved, and lost. I was afraid to share my feelings, good or bad, with anyone. This chapter in my life was full of disappointments and unfamiliarity. My dad initially thought it would be a good idea to send me to a middle school in Wausau, where he lived, but by day two, I did the unthinkable, at least for me—I ditched school. I never understood nor experienced mean girls at any previous school, but at this particular middle school, there was a group of girls, true "mean girls," who definitely wanted to live up to their reputation, so I was told. A girl I never met (my guardian angel) warned me that I would be beaten up after school, just because I was the "newbie" and to give me the message of where I "belonged." I left school sick, got approval to walk home, and hid in my closet from the world, so I thought, until my dad returned later that day. He did not make me go back to that school but did decide, because of his job and traveling, I needed to live with my aunt and uncle in that small unincorporated town in northern Wisconsin. It was for my protection, not knowing where my mom was, and being the youngest and only girl; my brothers were older and could take care of themselves. I was separated from the rest of my family, and unsure which would have been better, alone and scared or somewhat comfortable yet unfamiliar. Their daily routines were different, no longer dinner prayers or church services. I was grateful for what my aunt and uncle provided, but it wasn't "my family," "our normal." It was as though our once connected family turned into distance, confusion and personal survival. I was exposed to drugs and alcohol and witnessed lies and manipulation. This new life I was living felt like a car spinning out of control on black ice, with only the hope of it stopping before it crashed and burned.

The only thing that would stop this spinning and keep me from being drawn down a dark path, was to let go and let God. I believed God planted those seeds during the earlier years of my life, going to church, a Christian camp, and attending a parochial school, for the next chapter of my life to take place. I was in His hands. The good Lord was talking, and I listened. I clearly heard, *Be patient! Trust Me!* in whatever circumstance I was faced with.

My only survival was in my faith, in putting my life in God's hands, and in learning how to truly let go and let God.

The next four months seemed like the longest and hardest time of my life; I had no choices! Living with my aunt and uncle felt like an out-of-body experience. *Was I really separated from my own family?* Everything was different for this city girl; even washing my hair in a sink because they did not have a shower, just a large bathtub, which was difficult for this small-framed body to lean over without falling in. And, we certainly wouldn't hear the neighbors talking as the houses were so far apart. I often thought, if I screamed outside would anyone really hear me? I had never lived so far away from people before. It wasn't my "normal." The days became harder, and I longed to be with my mom. With a clear mind, and finally letting go and letting God, I asked my aunt for help in tracking down my mom's telephone number. The day my aunt handed me a piece of paper with my mom's telephone number on it was the first day in a very long time I felt alive again. That kind of excitement felt like the time years ago, when a friend and I ran down the street splashing through the rain puddles laughing, singing with no cares in the world. *What should I say? I'm excited and nervous at the same time. You've got this Mary, she's your mom, and she loves you. Don't worry about why she left, just tell her you miss her and want to see her. Okay... here I go.* The call wasn't awkward at all. Her voice seemed just as excited yet relieved as mine. We set up a date for me to travel from Rhinelander, Wisconsin to Waukesha, Wisconsin, for a visit during the holidays. My aunt and uncle dropped me off at the bus stop. I had been on city buses and school buses but never a large motorcoach before. It was a much more comfortable ride than bouncing up and down on a school bus. The seats were cushioned, and I could recline. It was about a four-hour bus ride, and all I could think about was, *would she look different when I saw her? Would she hug me and never let me go?* So many emotions went through my head it almost made me sick to my stomach with nerves. The bus ride went fine until we reached Milwaukee and the bus driver asked which of two stations I was getting off at. *Oh my goodness…I had no idea? I thought this was all figured out already when my aunt and uncle bought my ticket, and there would only be one place to stop; I certainly didn't know I was supposed to know this.* God gave me incredible strength, and I never panicked. I chose one of the stops and asked if I could use a telephone. I had written my mom's work telephone number down on a piece of paper and shoved it in my pocket. *Good thinking, Mary!* Although I knew she wouldn't be at work, I knew it was my only option of hope. My aunt was my guardian angel and helped me get here; God brought me here safely, I needed to keep my faith. I called her work and told them where I was. They were going to see if they could get a hold of her somehow.

Since I already loved to people-watch, sitting at the bus terminal killing time was just what I needed to do. It wasn't quite 30 minutes when my scan of people paid off. This beautiful woman walked through the door, and as I watched her head moving left to right, right to left, anxiously looking for someone, I stood up and ran as fast as I could. She was as beautiful as I remembered. And our hugs were so tight, neither one of us wanted to let go. It didn't matter what we did on this long weekend, as long as we were together. She lived in a small one-bedroom apartment; one so small I could stand in the middle of the room, spin around full circle and see the front door, living room, kitchen, dinette area, bathroom, and bedroom door. She had very basic furniture, a table to eat on, a used couch from St. Vincent de Paul's, and a mattress lying on the floor. I never cared what she had or didn't have, as long as we were together. Our conversations were endless; we laughed, cried, and reminisced about the good times. This memorable weekend went way too fast, and I didn't want to go back.

"Can't I just stay and live with you, Momma?" I begged.

"I'm in the process of getting a bigger apartment and more furniture. Let's make a plan, and once I get settled, you come back and live with me," my mom said convincingly.

Sad, but hopeful, I got back on the motorcoach and headed back to Rhinelander. I remember my thoughts spinning around quickly about what I needed to do and pack up so I could live with my mom again. The excitement was the only view I could see.

By January, I was back living with my mom; a separation I never wanted to go through again. These teen years were never what I had imagined, but I knew God had a plan and this was only part of my journey, not my destination. My life was in His hands.

While the New Year usually brings the presumption of new beginnings, do-overs, changes, goals, and new commitments, and this year was no different. More changes, a fresh start, new school, apartment living, and continuing to learn how to let go and let God, my faith grew stronger than this skinny brunette ever believed it could.

SO CLOSE AND YET SO FAR

It wasn't the inner city or out in the middle of nowhere but it was "home" with Mom. What seemed to be so close, was yet still too far, one-half mile too far to be exact, for this eighth grader to ride the bouncy school bus in this new city. No one knew my story. Although I should have been excited finally living with my mom, I was scared. Scared to start over again, especially when Mom and I pulled up to another new middle school for me to start that year. When we arrived, I panicked! I could not go inside; I couldn't let go of the car door. I did not want to leave my mom or meet anyone in fear of never seeing them again, especially my mom. She must have felt my pain; she never got mad at my emotions, but simply turned the car around and headed back home. We talked about my fears, and she said, "Tomorrow's another day, Honey." I felt relieved. Since I had a bad cold anyway, I just rested all day. The next day arrived on schedule, and I was even sicker than before; I stayed home again. By day three, Mom's encouraging words and reassurance that she herself would be there to pick me up later that day helped me to get over my fear of the unknown. I needed to believe and trust that her actions would follow her words. We walked together into the office where I met with a guidance counselor and again my mom assured me she would be back to pick me up. After encouraging conversations with the counselor, she walked me to my first class. I was quiet and sat towards the back. While waiting for the class to begin, this short blonde-haired girl sat down in front of me, snapped her head around so quickly I thought it would snap off her shoulder, and said, really bubbly, "Hi, my name is Patti-Jo, what's yours?" I just looked at her and thought, *are you kidding me, you're too bubbly for me. I hate my life and if you think I'm going to be friends with you, you've got another thing coming!* I just wanted to be left alone.

I got what I wished for, ALONE!

My mom started work early, and since we lived one-half mile short of riding the school bus, I had to walk to and from school. I didn't complain because I felt if I were alone, I wouldn't get disappointed or hurt. It was my morning time with God. He was the only one who understood how I felt inside. Just God and me walking to school! I liked our time together.

I loved the mornings, watching the sun rise as it came up over the houses, trees, and buildings on my walk to school. The street was not as busy as the inner-city streets I used to travel on to my previous elementary school, but the walk was familiar, with similar sidewalks and street lights. The traffic light turned green; I made a left and there it was, the biggest hill I had ever seen. Yes, I was a city girl, and this big hill was the closest thing to a mountain I would ever witness. In my own imagination, it was the size of the Rocky Mountains. It was a steep hill and a shortcut to my fourth new middle school I'd attended in five months. I slowly climbed straight up the middle, my calf muscles burned, as it was like climbing the "wall" of a mountain. I looked up and finally summited my "mountain." Instantly I began singing *"I'm on top of the orld lookin' down on creation, and the only explanation I can find, is the love that I've found ever since you've been around, your love's put me at the top of the world."* It was God's love that made me feel safe and "on top of the world."

DARKNESS TO LIGHT...HIS LIGHT

On my way home from school, when I reached the top of my "mountain," I would smile and thank God for making me feel on top of the world. Suddenly, my song was silenced and no longer was I feeling on top of the world. This hot, sunny, late-spring afternoon actually became a dark, cloudy, miserable day, for this skinny, freckle-faced fourteen-year-old. Sitting under a large oak tree, hiding from the world, so I thought, the pain was so fresh, and yet so deep already. Feeling confused, shocked, scared, and alone, my tears were uncontrollably drowning me.

Behind the tree I heard a voice, "Are you okay?" I was sobbing so hard I could barely speak. Her voice was gentle and kind, and as I looked up, I saw an angel. She had a loving and compassionate look in her eyes. A calm instantly came over me; I felt safe as though I could feel arms, from this large oak tree, wrapped around me.

She asked me if I believed in God. I replied, "Yes!" Although growing up and believing, attending church as a family, and praying before meals was great; this was different. A strong feeling of peace, security, and love, like never before, came over me.

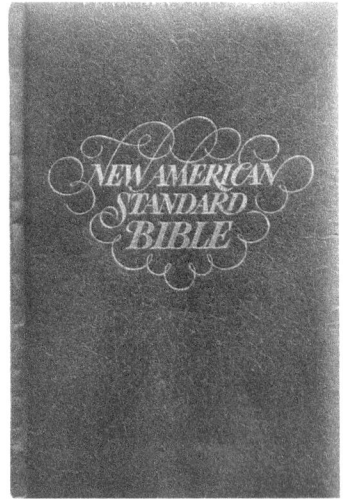

The gifted Bible, I still have and cherish

She spoke so openly about God, and how His incredible gift of love helps us through our pain. We talked about God, for what seemed like hours, when she asked me to walk with her to the Bible Institute. We went into her dorm room and there, she handed me her Bible, the one she wrote and highlighted in and obviously cherished. Handing it to me, without hesitation, after writing her name and phone number on the cover, she hugged me and said, "God loves you, and you can call me anytime."

Later in the week, I saw her sitting under that same oak tree, reading the Bible with her boyfriend. We smiled at each other, as I sat under another tree reading the Bible she gave me, feeling safe and secure. I felt protected, holding the gifted Bible and knowing this angel was sitting under that oak tree watching over me.

It was as though knowing this angel was there, sitting under that tree, gave me comfort. Then, she was gone. Every new day, I looked for her, scanned the hillside and looked next to every tree, hoping to find her watching over me. Where did she go? Did she really exist? I sat next to the oak tree, head in my hands, cried, prayed and begged for my angel to come back, protect me and give me the strength I needed.

Ellen Bennett never knew the day we first met, was the day I was sexually abused by a family member, and the day God changed my life. I kept the secret and trusted God to protect me. I felt safer when I heard my mom say, "It's called tough love," as she kicked my oldest brother out of the apartment due to his bad choices.

I witnessed my selfless mother's faith through her words and actions. I couldn't wait to grow up and be just like her, yet I was scared my deep secret would keep me from having a boyfriend, ever getting married, or having children. The few boys I dated broke up with me, without giving a reason. Feeling ugly, unloved and never good enough, I cried myself to sleep many nights. Whenever my mom knew I was feeling down, she would walk me into a room with a mirror and say, "Look at yourself, and repeat after me, You ARE beautiful, you ARE holy, and you ARE loved. You need to believe what I see and how God made you!"

Although I had so much pain inside after the abuse, between my mom's affirmations and my angel Ellen, they opened my eyes to see how God was working in my life and how much He unconditionally loves me. This love in my heart made me feel like I truly was on top of the world. I sang that song every day while I walked to school, realizing, with God, all things ARE possible. God is the one and only, who made me feel like, "I'm on top of the world" as I looked down on His creation, when I let go and let God.

Life isn't easy; let's face it. We can say we forgive, trust, let go and let God, but just being human sometimes, makes it actually so difficult to do. I do know that having FAITH, even as small as the size of a mustard seed, is enough. It's enough for our eyes to see how much God loves us, how He can transform our lives to make us feel "on top of the world," and how He gives us the gift of fortitude, and to stand up for what is right.

Let us not become weary in doing good, for at the proper time we will reap a harvest if we do not give up. Galatians 6:9 NIV

CHAPTER TWO

UNDERSTANDING

Relate all truths to one's supernatural purpose

Let Go

and

Let God

Commit to the Lord whatever you do, and he will establish your plans.

Proverbs 16:3 NIV

HOW WOULD YOU MEASURE YOUR FAITH?

Would you say your faith was at least the size of a mustard seed? Is it easy for you to let go and let God?

He replied, "Because you have so little faith. Truly I tell you, if you have faith as small as a mustard seed, you can say to this mountain, 'Move from here to there,' and it will move.
Nothing will be impossible for you." Matthew 17:20 NIV

Letting go and letting God would be easy to understand if having the teeniest, tiniest amount of faith was all it took to get through life. It is! However, what sounds easy sometimes is the most difficult to do. We all want some control in our lives; whether hoping others will see or do things our way; or maybe waiting for God to answer prayers the way we want them to be answered.

Have you ever felt that way?

Our anxieties, burdens, mental and emotional abuse, and the lack of forgiveness, are examples of the heavy crosses we carry throughout our lives. This weight is what God wants us to let go of and let Him control. He wants us to put our lives in His hands. Satan wants us to compare, "My cross is heavier than yours!" which steals our joy and the plan God has for us.

Whenever there was a little joy, that little glimmer of light in my life, Satan made my cross a little heavier, which felt like he was adding a heavy brick to each step I took along my journey, just to see how much I could handle or to test my faith. I felt like Job in the Bible; my faith was constantly being tested. I let go and trusted God through the pain of my parents' divorce and my secret of sexual abuse at fourteen but, I wasn't completely letting go and letting God, and I didn't understand that having faith, even the size of a mustard seed was enough, since I allowed Satan to keep the weight of my cross heavy enough, to keep this annoying back and forth game going.

Can you relate to being tested in your faith?

I felt broken from my parents' divorce; I no longer shared a room with my beloved grandma; and the weight of the abuse was too heavy to bear at times. I could go visit my grandma, but she lived too far from me. It was no longer like the days when I would come home from school, sit on the edge of the bed, and we'd have a nonstop dialogue about our day. She was a witness to the Kingdom, a strong Christian woman, not only loving the Lord, but everyone around her. Between Grandma and Mom, both selfless, caring, and compassionate examples in my life, I wanted to grow up and be just like them. I no longer wanted to allow my fears to define me or allow Satan to steal that joy from my heart.

Two years after the abuse, while sitting in a high school classroom, a pass was brought in for me. *WHAT? I never get a pass. What did I do wrong? I feel sick. I'm scared.* My head was spinning as I wondered what could I have possibly done wrong? *I was known as the "good girl."* I walked into the front office, and there stood my mom. She received a phone call of my grandmother's passing and wanted to be the first to tell me, knowing how close my grandmother and I were. I was shaking and felt like someone socked me in the stomach. I not only lost my grandmother, but the one person who never judged me or anyone, the one I shared anything and everything with…the one who taught me how to be a selfless person.

When I returned to school later that week, a classmate asked me where I was. I said, "My grandmother passed away."

He said, "It was only your grandmother, that's what they do, get old and die!"

"WHAT?!"

"She was NOT just my grandmother, she was my best friend." *How could he say that? He obviously did not have the same relationship with his grandmother.*

Reflecting back: I learned so much from her. Witnessing her selflessness, caring and kind heart, her love for the Lord, and compassion for others. She was creative and poetic. She saved every greeting card she ever received, cut out the images, poems, or pictures on the front of the card, and glue them to a large piece of cardboard or plastic and then make placemats. We would also take the city bus downtown, (she didn't drive), when we lived on the north side of Milwaukee. We would stop downtown Milwaukee on Wisconsin Avenue, shop, have lunch, and then return on the bus in the late afternoon. I spent my summers at her church day center, making crafts and spending a lot of time with the elderly. Sometimes it reminded me of the time I went to Camp LuWiSoMo. I loved it there; it gave me a sense of belonging, love in my heart, and compassion for others.

I cherish every lesson I learned and blessing I received from my grandmother. My love for her was so deep; my heart still aches for her today.

FAITH, HOPE, AND LOVE

My grandma used to tell me to trust God, and He would put someone in my life at just the right time. Well, He did! Joy rekindled the heart for this hazel-eyed brunette when I fell in love and got married at twenty-one years old. Letting go and letting God wasn't always easy. I still found myself running from my fears, holding tight to "doing" instead of "being," and losing myself and what I wanted in life.

Besides marriage, I wanted children. I hoped and prayed that one day God would bless me with a child. By the age of twenty-five, I suffered two miscarriages; whether planned or not, the unwelcomed comments "It's not a baby at that time," or "Since you weren't planning it, it's God's way to say you weren't ready" and then watching my sisters-in-law carry their babies to full term. It was difficult at times to be happy and act like that internal pain did not exist, especially around my sisters-in-law, but the pain was real and did exist! I wanted what they had, and I became jealous and envious until I finally listened to the still small voice, "Let go Let God!" That was my constant reminder; He was in control, not me. I needed to trust Him. My prayers were answered and God's sense of humor with a "three times a charm" pregnancy was my state of euphoria. I felt truly blessed. I was unstoppable. Satan was NOT going to steal my joy this time!

Does Satan try to steal your joy when life is going well? Do you ever feel like your faith is constantly being tested?

I was happy and finally pregnant when I received a call from my doctor. He wanted me to see him so we could talk privately.

"Just tell me what's going on!" I insisted.

Reluctantly he said, "Mary, you need to see a specialist. Your baby may be deformed, have health issues, and you'll need to make a decision." *What does that mean, make a decision? What kind of decision? I learned to trust God before…so why stop now?*

The decision was easy, I replied, "I am keeping my baby and will trust God."

"I still recommend you seeing a specialist," my doctor insisted.

Unfortunately, the specialist appointment was on the same brisk fall day we moved into our new home. My mom insisted on taking me. I was nervous. My hands were sweaty, and I was still adamant about my decision. *So why am I here?* We walked into a small office with a round table surrounded by hanging certificates and accolades. "Before I do any testing, I need to ask some personal family history questions. Let's begin with your mom. How many pregnancies have you had?" the doctor asked. There was a long pause, and the deafening silence scared me. I knew about several miscarriages but what secret was she keeping? I looked across the table; tears streamed down her cheeks. Looking quite confused, the doctor said, "I'll leave you two alone," as he walked out. She cried harder and said, "I thought this secret would be mine until the day I died."

"Mom, what secret?" I anxiously and hesitantly asked.

"At sixteen years old, I had a baby who died ten days after he was born of a hole in his heart. You can't tell anyone!" She wouldn't share details, so I wondered if she was raped. After telling the doctor, it was up to her if she wanted to share her secret with anyone else.

The doctor then proceeded with an ultrasound and then an amniocentesis (removing a small amount of fluid from the sac around the baby in the womb) to check for birth defects, genetic problems (especially since my mom lost a baby with a hole in its heart), lung development and any infections. I was still adamant about keeping my baby and putting the unknown in God's hands. While preparing for the celebration of the birth of our Lord and Savior at Christmas, we received a phone call from the doctor.

"The test results are final, and your baby does not have any heart, lung or genetic issues nor birth defects," he excitedly shared.

Although my decision was already made, I did have a sigh of relief knowing the baby would be healthy.

When my April 2nd due date passed, I became more anxious and ready for this new bundle of joy to arrive. *All in God's timing,* I reminded myself over and over again. The nesting stage set in and the wait began. On Saturday, April 14th, I went into labor and after 18 hrs of what should have been painful, and no progression, the doctor became concerned. He went back and read through my records and on Easter Sunday he said, "Since you do not feel the pain of the contraction, even after receiving Pitocin, we need to know why and do an emergency cesarean section. I became scared at first but trusted the doctor and put everything in God's

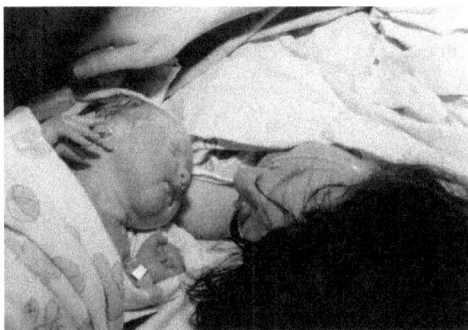

hands. God blessed us that Easter Sunday with a beautiful and healthy baby girl, who was given the name Michelle. The "why" I couldn't give birth naturally was because the doctor discovered I had a bicornuate uterus, which means a heart-shaped uterus, causing each side to push down independently during contractions, not allowing my cervix to dilate.

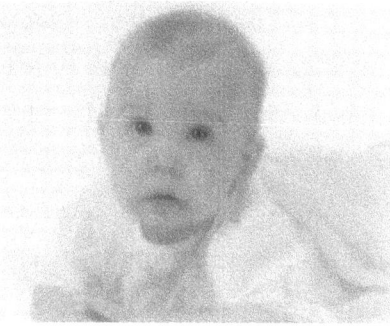

I couldn't thank God enough. He answered my prayers and life was good. Unbeknownst to me, a storm was brewing on this beautiful, late spring sunny day, while my precious Easter gift was sound asleep. Startled by a knock on the door, the dark cloud, I thought had dissipated, reappeared after 11 years. I felt my heart pounding as the door opened, and once again I was face-to-face with the man who robbed me of my innocence, who now insisted on meeting my little girl. He made me promise to tell no one, and I hadn't, so why didn't he just leave me alone?

Although I began feeling sick and scared, I knew I needed to remain calm, as I had no idea what this large man, a family member who I once trusted, would do to either one of us. I trusted God to keep Michelle sleeping safely and me calm. I heard every second ticking by on the clock that hung on the kitchen wall, *tick, tick, tick…*I watched the big hand move from one minute to the next as his sleep apnea caused him to dose off while he sat and waited. *Okay God, I'm waiting, now what do I do?* I wondered. The sounds became deafening in my head. Actual minutes felt like hours. His body jerked, waking him, as I calmly convinced him to leave.

"She could sleep all day," I said.

My prayers were answered. He got up and left before Michelle woke up. I immediately locked the door behind him and prayed he would never return. What seemed to be the longest minutes of my life were just enough time to talk him into leaving. I sat in fear of him coming back and couldn't hold on to this secret any longer. No more dark secrets. I called my mom and told her everything.

She didn't seem as shocked as I thought she would have. She confronted him, only to hear, "Mary needs to get over it; it was a long time ago, and I was on drugs." As though that was a good excuse for his bad behavior. Unfortunately, it was a topic never to be talked about again.

LIFE AFTER DEATH

Life was going great; I was married, living in a nice home, gifted with a beautiful daughter after suffering two miscarriages, and then I was pregnant again. I prayed for a healthy pregnancy and healthy baby. *Ok, I admit, I not only prayed for a healthy baby, but selfishly I prayed for a boy.* Waiting for that three-month mark, the "if I make it to three months nothing can happen to this baby" timeframe, before sharing the exciting news with family and friends about our little blessing on the way. Finally, the news was out! Everyone was elated, and the celebrations and planning began.

Wait...no! Stop this! It can't be! I refuse to accept this. I started spotting. The doctor immediately told me to put my feet up, rest, and it would be ok, not to worry. How could I not worry? I tried to relax and rest my body. Then the unthinkable nightmare began. I woke up in the middle of the night from what felt like menstrual cramps. I was in shock and refused to accept this was happening to my body. I went into labor that night; it was the beginning of my second trimester. It was a horrific experience. By the time I got to the hospital, I was hemorrhaging, and my blood pressure had dropped. *What was happening? Chaos everywhere. Was I dying? I heard, "Oh my God, I've never seen anything like this!" as the doctor yelled, "Get her out of here!"* Then, silence, I was out, and no more pain was felt.

What just happened to me? Was I dead? Was I having an out-of-body experience?

I opened my eyes, my body shaking, and I wondered what just took place? There I was, lying in my hospital bed, feeling glued to the bed, motionless and broken. I reached down and placed my hands gently on my belly, as an endless flow of tears ran down my cheeks. I felt empty and lost. I felt like my entire life was ripped out of me, and the knot in my stomach felt like someone just punched me in the gut.

I was waiting to hear, "You're ok! I'll be right back to discharge you!"

I'm not ok! I'll never be ok! What now? How do I go on?

Losing another child was heart wrenching, and I didn't know how to go on. I was angry, no longer wanting to wear my smile, be nice, or go out of my way for anyone. I just wanted to crawl under a rock, and have everyone leave me alone. *How do I let go and let God with such anger?*

As I waited in my frozen state of mind, to hear the infamous, "You're ok to be discharged, go forward…be happy…blah blah blah," this woman who looked like a nurse, walked into my hospital room. Our eyes met, no words were spoken as she walked directly towards me with a gentle compassionate smile as she tightly wrapped her loving arms around me. She was my angel, my miracle, and gift from God. At that moment, I felt nothing but peace and love. Her hug was warm and embraced me as though God was holding me tightly in His own arms. I knew in that moment, God sent this compassionate loving woman to me, so I would know everything would be ok, and in time I would move forward and let go and let God.

I received God's mercy and the gift of peace, hope in my heart, and understood I had to move forward and be my best self, be the "ME" God created. My two-year-old baby girl, Michelle, was waiting at home for me to take care of her. God gave me an abundant amount of strength, strength I never thought I had, to focus on my baby girl, be the best mom I could, and continue to let go and trust God.

Life never seems complicated when we let go and let God. Why try to control a journey that God has already mapped out? When we listen to the still small voice, the Holy Spirit's guidance, and live in the moment, life is beautiful, and our paths become our journey, not our destination.

Trust in the LORD with all your heart and do not lean on your own understanding. In all your ways acknowledge Him, and He will make your paths straight. Proverbs 3:5-6 NIV

MIRACLES DO HAPPEN

The rollercoaster of personal control and insecure mind games, keeps us from listening and believing miracles do happen. I thought I was letting go and trusting God, as He was guiding me down His path for His purpose; I instead was questioning not listening. God used my little girl to tell me the good news, but my mind was allowing Satan to tell me it wasn't possible.

It was the beginning of summer, and the clear blue sky was as far as the naked eye could see. The day was more perfect for a round of golf, not walking into a golf store. Michelle immediately ran over to this large bin and picked up baby blue golf tees that say, "It's a boy" and handed them to me while she said, "Mommy, baby boy!" At first, I gently took them from her, placed them back in the bin and said, "We don't need them, Honey. We don't know anyone having a baby boy." Again, she picked them up, handed them to me and insisted, "Mommy…baby boy!" This time I got slightly annoyed, "PLEASE, just put them back!" as we finished this back and forth game of disappointment for me.

The next week, I started to feel sick. I must have a bug; I thought. I was scheduled for my follow-up checkup with my doctor from my miscarriage. They did the usual urine test, but when the doctor came in, he smiled and said, "Congratulations you're pregnant again!" I was in shock, very excited, but in shock. I had no idea. Yes, I was late, but that wasn't unusual for me.

Then, everything my little girl told me raced through my head. *Could this be? Could this really be a baby boy? Why was I not listening? God was using her to tell me, and I wasn't listening!* Because of prior complications, the doctor insisted on doing an ultrasound to make sure everything was normal. Curiosity lead me to asking if I was having a boy, and I kept the findings to myself until the day the baby was born.

God's plan always seemed to throw me for a loop. *Why would I ever question Him?* Flexibility, change, and new beginnings became my way of life. This secret little boy wasn't due until early

March. During my last trimester, our family had an unexpected move to Michigan, and God chose the quaint town of Jackson as our new home. It was one of those towns I never thought existed, one where a neighbor invited my daughter Michelle and me over for a small neighborhood get-together. The town wasn't the only thing quaint; the host neighbor lived three houses down from me and had invited all the surrounding neighbors to join us for coffee, tea, juice, and wonderful homemade desserts. The host had chairs gathered around the living room so no one would feel left out. Everyone went around the room and introduced themselves. They were all Christian women from all denominations, and a couple who actually went to the same church our family just joined. Most of the ladies were elderly and one younger woman, in particular, stood out. I learned she lived diagonally behind me, was about five to ten years older, and just as happy to meet someone around her own age. I loved the elderly women, but I was also hoping for playmates for my children, or possibly a babysitter. The younger neighbor, Pam, gave me a hug and said, "If there is anything you need, please let me know."

This warm welcome was definitely something new for me and a real blessing.

This move also lead me to finding a new doctor in Michigan.

I'm sure glad I had over a month before my delivery date, especially with this blustery February weather! BREAKING NEWS…everyone was encouraged to stay home and off the roads. The breaking news came just in time. My husband's business travel plans turned into an office day. While lying on the couch, I looked out the living room window at the beautiful large snowflakes accumulating. It was so breathtaking. Suddenly, out of nowhere, my little girl came up next to me, put her hand gently on my belly, and said, "Mommy, baby today!"

"No, Honey, Mommy has another month to go." She insisted again. Before too long, I started to feel sick. Contractions started and the doctor insisted I go to the hospital. *Of course, my new doctor was on vacation and thought he would be back in plenty of time before my March delivery date.* Not the case, and now I had someone else, someone new I had to trust.

My mom planned on coming over in March to help me with the children, but now what? I immediately called my mom, who lived in Wisconsin, to give her the update.

"I'm on my way, Honey. I'll be there in about six hours!" excitedly replied my mom.

Who will watch Michelle? Instantly I thought of Pam. I remembered what she said, and for just meeting someone, it felt like we knew each other forever. It was God's plan for us to meet at that welcoming social. I called Pam, and she graciously accepted to watch Michelle until my mom came. When we dropped Michelle off at Pam's, her demeanor was surprisingly calm and comfortable. It was almost as if she knew that she was relieving me of the stresses of the weather, the baby coming early, and my mom not being there yet.

I put my trust in God, met my new doctor, and after the examination he asked, "Do you believe in fate?"

"Yes! Why?" I asked.

"Something is wrong, and we need to do an emergency caesarean section," he told me.

The thought of losing another child was too difficult. Repeatedly hearing the still small voice, *TRUST ME! Let go and let God!* I trusted and was blessed with a premature little boy. But, before I had a chance to hold my precious gift, like an eagle swooping down protecting his fallen eaglet from prey, my little angel was taken away from me.

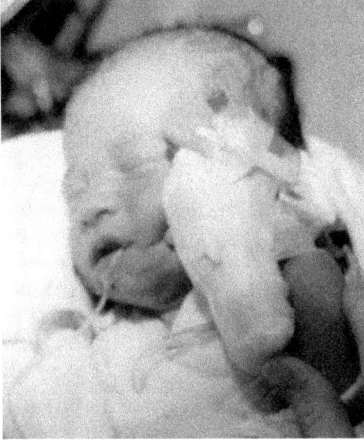

"I'm sorry, your son is very sick; his lungs aren't fully developed, and he was born with pneumonia. We don't think he will make it through the night." They swooped him away from me, and I had to put him in God's hands. I had to let go and trust Him.

My husband called our new church and without hesitation, the Pastor, Father John Kettelberger came directly to the hospital to see us. He asked to see our little Nik, baptized him, and then returned to my hospital bedside. He held my hand, waited, and prayed with me for hours. It was all we could do at the time; it was completely out of our control. Nik was in God's hands. My heart hurt watching him in the neonatal intensive care unit (NICU) with a feeding tube down his throat and his little arm secured so the IV wouldn't come out. As the doctors were making plans to get a helicopter ready to transport him to Ann Arbor Hospital, Father John left and said he would continue to pray for strength and healing for Nik. Father John was our angel. After he left, the RUSH of getting Nik on the helicopter came to a halt.

"There was a slight change in his numbers!" the medical team announced.

They said, if his numbers continued to improve, they would keep him in Jackson in the NICU, otherwise by morning he would be

Feeding Nik for the first time

transported to Ann Arbor. The power of prayer was just that… POWERFUL PRAYERS ANSWERED! This little guy hung on, and although the next week was the longest week of my life, he slowly made progress, and by Valentine's Day, he was out of the NICU. By the second week, he was able to go home. I let go and trusted God!

Wait for the Lord; be strong, and let your heart take courage; wait for the Lord! Psalm 27:14

DAILY BLESSINGS

God opened my eyes and heart to be grateful for everything and treat each day as a precious gift taking nothing for granted. I put my life in God's hands. While Nik became stronger, Michelle became the older protective sister. Although she turned three the year Nik was born, it was as though she understood how sick he was,

and was just as protective as I was. Nik was going to know how much he was loved, whether he understood it or not; there was no stopping us!

Spring has always been one of my favorite times of the year, and that year, Nik made it even better. The sweet smell of the blooming flowers was more aromatic, and tulips popping out of the ground were brighter. This was a true sense of "a breath of fresh air." Our neighborhood in Michigan was the complete opposite of the one I grew up in. The houses were further apart, and there were no sidewalks in our subdivision. If you went for a walk, you walked on the road. Michelle and I strolled Nik around the neighborhood, and upon our return a large mobile home pulled up in the neighbor's driveway. As we curiously watched them park, the door then opened and an elderly woman stepped down and glanced over at us, looking just as curious as we were. Then an elderly man followed behind. Michelle was so excited to greet them, just like the other neighbors greeted us upon our arrival, she took off running towards the elderly woman and shouted, "Hi Grandmama" and gave her a big hug. Anyone would have thought we knew her our entire life. It was the first day of having our adopted grandparents live next door, especially since we lived so far from their own grandparents. The elderly couple was Don and Suzanne. It was the beginning of a lifelong friendship.

IT'S A SMALL WORLD

We were very blessed to have such loving people surround us, and I was fortunate enough to be a stay-at-home mom at the time. It always seemed so peaceful, quiet, and neighbors naturally watched out for each other. It seemed like everyone knew someone, whether directly in the neighborhood or across town, the church and community were all connected. It was definitely a "small world," *or one large family under God's roof.* Through these connections, I would occasionally babysit for a little extra cash. I joined a playgroup which consisted of six families. The moms took turns hosting breakfast/snack/drinks while the children played together and the moms socialized. Through this, we created a babysitting co-op group and exchanged tickets for watching each other's children, allowing us to have adult time away, without having to pay a babysitter. It was certainly a WIN WIN for all of us.

LIFE-CHANGING GOLF GAME

I earned enough tickets to join a women's golf league. This was no ordinary Tuesday or a typical golf game. It was a teacher and lesson that would change my life forever.

Our women's golf league consisted mostly of teachers on summer break, but for me, it was my adult getaway. Luck was in my favor; my golf game was going well and unbeknownst to me; the day was just about to get better.

As I walked to the next tee box, I overheard one of the women saying, "I know, I need to get out more often, but my schedule is too busy." As they got closer, my friend introduced me to the busy stranger. We continued our walk to the tee box, and our conversation was like two friends who hadn't seen each other in years, getting caught up on life. There was a definite connection and reason why we met. Because most of the women on the league were school teachers, she naturally thought I was one as well. So, she asked the inevitable question, "What do you teach?"

"I'm not a teacher, I'm just a stay-at-home mom." I replied.

I should have said, "I'm not JUST a stay-at-home mom, I AM a teacher...to my own children! I read to them, plan daily activities, and am constantly teaching them something new. But that is not what came out. I'm just a stay-at-home mom, did!"

The busy stranger not only taught at an elementary school, but taught fifth grade religious education classes on Sunday, at the same church I belonged to. She was looking to try something new that year and team-teach the religious education class. With her demanding schedule, she thought team-teaching might allow her some freedom. Her plan would allow the teachers to alternate and teach every other session, which was once a month, since the students met every other week. She said, "I think you'd be great at it! What do you think?"

How did she know I would be great at it? We never met before, and she knew nothing about me. Although, we did talk like we knew each other our entire lives.

All of a sudden, I felt this strong, yet calming sense, to excitedly say, "Yes! Absolutely! I would love to!"

I had a little over a month to prepare for my first day. I was very excited to do so. It felt right, normal, and comfortable for me. I was completely putting this in God's hands.

Although I thought I was calm, cool, and collected during my preparation, I became a little nervous walking into that classroom the first day. I always wanted to be a teacher and couldn't believe this was a dream come true. Because the classroom was diverse, I believed I learned from the students just as much as they learned from me. My favorite lesson was about creating a news headline story; "If you could make a difference in the world, what would you do and what would it look like?"

And of course, being the teacher, I had to create a sample story to show the class. My headline story was: "No one was Homeless this Thanksgiving." In my mind, it would look like this: all the homeless would be brought into a large banquet hall, with tables set in white linen table clothes, with silverware, and each person would have a different patterned plate, representing our differences, one family under God. And, of course we would eat family style. That was never a real headline story, but teaching the lesson taught everyone an impactful message; we are all different in many ways and have our own story to tell. That lesson created a lot of discussion and understanding about our differences and how not to judge nor compete—to just be the person God created each of us to be.

That year went fast and by team-teaching, the busy stranger was able to free up her time. By the following year, she wanted her fulltime teaching position back. It was not only a dream come true for me, but an opportunity to experience and share my gifts from God. That busy stranger and the new Tuesday morning golf league was the best lesson, and it changed my life.

SERVING OTHERS

This change inside of me personally impacted my life and serving others; I wanted to do more. I contacted Father John, one of the four Vincentian Priests (Vincentian's founded by St. Vincent de Paul in 1625, arrived in the United States in 1816, serving the poor and abandoned) at Queen of the Miraculous Medal Church in Jackson. More wisdom, understanding, and doors to my future were opened as Father John and I discussed serving opportunities for me through our church and community.

I joined the Women's Guild and belonged to a "Circle" which was a group of women who met monthly and talked about ways to give back, help others, and our community. Throughout the year we did just that, gave back. The holidays became more meaningful to me. Two holidays in particular—Christmas and Easter both have a deeper memory for me. In preparation of Christmas, I was honored to be asked to put on the Christmas trees lights, displayed on each side of the alter, three on each side to be exact, which took hours. Suzanne or "Grandmama" as Michelle called her, insisted on watching the children so I could decorate the trees. Father John got the supply of lights and ladder for me, locked the church, so no one would come in or startle me, and periodically checked in to see if I needed anything.

I quickly learned, it wasn't about putting the Christmas lights on the trees at all, it was my vacation from the world around me, a sacred place, where no one could hurt me, judge me, or fill my head with negativity. It was a blessing, a gift from God. And, an understanding that the Father in this house loved me unconditionally, without judgment, and He was forgiving.

Forgiveness is what comes to mind when I think of Easter. Although as a child, we went to Sunrise Service at our church, Easter was more about looking for a hidden Easter basket filled with candy, colored eggs, and maybe a small toy. As an adult, and being taught Easter was a time to celebrate the resurrection of Jesus, who died on the cross for our sins, this particular year was different. Easter wasn't just one day. It was a Holy week. And, on Holy Thursday, a day to celebrate the Last Supper, this year was different, with more meaning. I worked closely with Father John, planned a time to bring more of the community together, and coordinated the Seder Meal (a reenactment of the Passover Meal). That Holy week not only changed me, but increased my deeper internal level of understanding of what Jesus went through that week.

The light of Christ was burning brighter inside of me. I felt urged to do even more. Father John introduced me to Sister Ann, who personally came to my house, which made it easier for me, having children, and a husband who traveled every week, and she trained me to be a Homebound Minister. Each minister received names of people to visit weekly. I took the Eucharist to the Homebound and prayed with them. The best part was that I did not need to worry about a babysitter; both Nik and Michelle could go with me at any given time. Most often, because Michelle was in school, it was Nik and me. Both children shared my excitement spending time with the with the homebound; whether we walked into a nursing home, apartment or residence, we knew we were serving God by seeing the excitement on the faces of all of the people we visited. I felt the warmth in my heart, another incredible life lesson which continued to bless our lives.

When we put our lives in God's hands, He shows us patience, gives us wisdom, strength, and teaches us to let go and let God!

THE POWER OF PRAYER = A SAFE TRIP

God's plan for our family was another opportunity to move. This time we moved from Michigan to Arizona. A few days prior to our last Christmas in our Jackson, Michigan home, a car pulled into the driveway and out came one of the elderly homebound women we would visit. She walked up to the door and said, "I have something special for you Mary, as you have been an angel in my life." I didn't know she knew where I lived. She handed me a wrapped gift in an open cardboard box. I gently unwrapped the gift of a silver ceramic angel and on the bottom, she wrote "To Mary from Regina on 12/21/1996." She hugged me, thanked me again and turned around as though her mission was accomplished. I never saw Regina again. She indeed was the angel in my life.

When I said we put things in God's hands, I truly meant it. One morning, Michelle asked Nik and I to go with her into her bedroom; at which time she asked us to sit down, hold hands while she prayed. She prayed for safety and for someone to buy our home. That week, during a terrible ice storm, our home was the only one on our block with electricity, and when the phone rang unfortunately my mind raced to hoping it wasn't a call about an accident. To my surprise, it was the realtor with great news and said, "YOUR HOUSE IS SOLD!" I stood shocked for a quick moment and then turned, grabbed and hugged Michelle and said, "Our prayers were answered; our house is sold. Michelle was our little angel. The following week, the school psychologist at Queens, the parochial school Michelle attended, called me to talk about Michelle's school drawings, and we discussed our move to Arizona. I wondered what she could tell me about our move to Arizona?

"Michelle is very direct when she talks," said the school psychologist.

"Michelle doesn't say words like 'I think' or 'I feel,'" she added.

Michelle told the school psychologist that we were moving to Arizona and would be in an accident while driving to Arizona but no one would get hurt. My heart was heavy with such mixed emotions. It was a bittersweet day; we were excited for a new journey to where the sun shines 365 days a year, and sad to say goodbye to Don and Suzanne. They were like family. I told them we would stay in touch and always be a part of their lives.

It was difficult not to be excited about our journey ahead, 365 days of sunshine a year, and the weather hot and dry. As this bittersweet day came to an end. I'm not sure who cried harder me or Suzanne. Don had dreams of taking Nik golfing and fishing and they both wanted to watch the children grow up. The more I heard what they wanted, the harder it was to say goodbye to our adopted grandparents, Don and Suzanne.

We didn't forget the serious information the school psychologist shared with us. We had the car blessed and prayed as often as we could during the trip from Michigan to Arizona. By the time we arrived at our new home, black fluid was splattered all over the back of my Jeep Cherokee.

When the mechanic looked at it, and heard we just drove all the way from Michigan, he said, "You are lucky to be alive, that is brake fluid!" We WERE lucky! We put our trust in God's hands and took Michelle's concerns seriously. It was as though she was my guardian angel; she did tell me I was having a boy, and he was coming into the world earlier than expected; and she prayed for our house to sell, which it did in an ice storm.

Understanding Michelle's supernatural purpose led us to continued trust and putting our lives in God's hands.

What would you have done?

Trust in the Lord with all thine heart; and lean not unto thine own understanding. Proverbs 3:5 KJV

Scrapbook

Michelle, grandpa Don, Nik, and grandmamma Suzanne

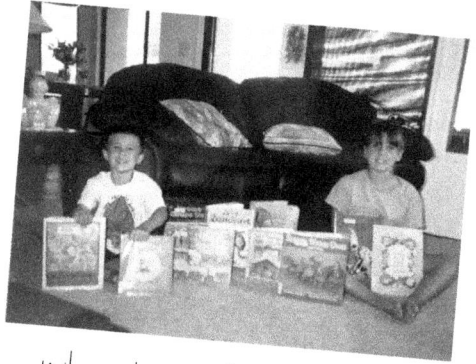

Nik and Michelle display their weekly summer Library reads, while staying cool from the Arizona heat. (The guardian Angel is watching over them)

At Don's grave with Suzanne

Father John & Suzanne taking a Selfie

Father John visits
Milwaukee

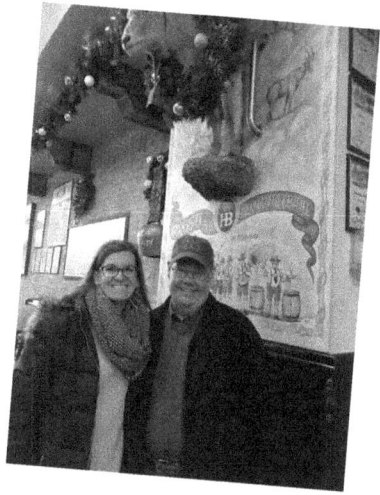

With Father John in New York

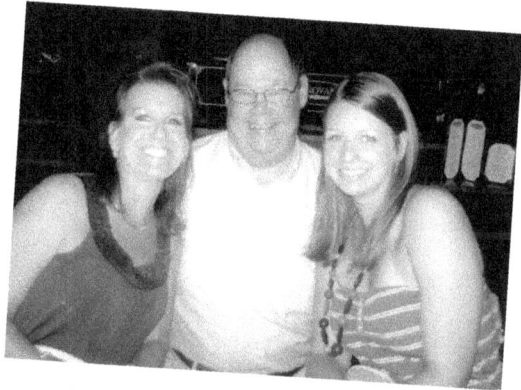

With Michelle and Father John

Michelle & Father John at St. John's
University, NYC

CHAPTER THREE

FEAR OF THE LORD

Aware of the glory and majesty of God…
the beginning of wisdom

Hope

The fear of the Lord is the beginning of wisdom, and knowledge of the Holy One is understanding.

Proverbs 9:10 NIV

A NEW CHAPTER...NEW ADVENTURES...NEW LIFE

We put our trust in God's hands and made it to the next chapter of our lives. My fear of the Lord (wisdom of loving Him and avoiding evil) is knowing God had a plan and a purpose for me. My faith was growing stronger and deeper than I had ever imagined. Believe...there is hope! Faith, even as small as the size of a mustard seed, is enough!

My future was no longer going to be defined by the pain of the abuse, the loneliness in my heart, or my past, but by the love of Christ in my heart, living for Him and allowing Christ to continue making me feel like I'm on top of the world. I now see the world differently. I see God turning my messes into messages, my trials into triumphs, and any broken mentality into a breakthrough. My challenges become blessings. Had I not gone through "this" (whatever "this" was) I might not have seen that (whatever "that" was). I have newfound hope!

With every new move, my mom would encourage me to "get lost" as she reminded me one is never lost, just headed in different directions. So, on this hot but not scorching Arizona sunny morning, I took my mom's advice and Nik and I decided to explore Arizona, after we dropped Michelle off at school, and "get lost." Nik was too young for Pre-K yet so our timing to go exploring was perfect.

Phoenix reminded me of a gigantic shallow bowl with mountains all-encompassing the city. We lived in North Glendale, and I decided to drive west.

"Nik, let's go explore, 'get lost' and head towards the mountains," I said excitedly.

"YEAH!" Nik replied.

"Wait, I need to get something, Mommy!" Nik said as he ran back into the house.

Nik was notorious for having to bring some type of airplane with every car ride. He definitely knew and loved planes.

"Only two planes!" I reminded him. Otherwise, we'd have a car full.

"Okay, Mommy, now I'm ready to get lost!" as he excitedly said while making jet sounds.

We started out taking Bell Road straight West and purposely stayed off the freeway so we could see more sights. Once we drove away from the city and busyness, it was like a whole new world opened up. There were wide-open spaces all around us.

"Smell that?" I asked Nik.

"It smells sweet, Mommy," Nik replied.

"They're citrus orchards Honey. I'm glad I took Grandma's advice too Nik, this drive is breathtaking."

As we passed El Mirage, Surprise and continued towards the mountain range we came across this sign, "Wildlife World Zoo, Aquarium and Safari Park ahead."

We followed the sign and came upon a zoo like nothing I've ever seen before. It was more real-looking than the city zoos I was familiar with. From what we could see from the outside, it looked like the wildlife were living in the wild, their own environment.

"That looks like a fun place to come back and visit with your sister, Nik!" I said.

Nik agreed.

While we continued driving down Northern Parkway, we heard this loud, fast jet engine sound. *What in the world was that? I wondered.*

"MOMMY IT'S A JET!!" Nik yelled out excitedly.

Nik has always loved airplanes and just so happened to grab two Air Force jets before we left the house.

We followed the direction of the jets as they began their descent and saw another sign, "Luke Air Force Base ahead." At this point, I'm not sure who was more excited.

We found a parking lot and literally sat watching the airplanes land. The parking lot was in line of the landing strip. We could see the engine flames, even in the bright, sunny, hot daytime and could feel the engine thrust in our chests.

"Hey, Nik, I see the McDonald arch. How would you like a Happy Meal, and we can come back and continue watching the jets for a little longer?"

"YEAH! Thank you, Mommy,!" Nik excitedly replied.

This became Mommy and Nik's new little weekly get-a-way, a Happy Meal and jets, two of Nik's favorites.

BELIEVE IT!

It was another scorching, 110-plus-degree day in Arizona when a loud screeching sound was heard outside our house. A car flew over the curb and down into a beautiful, green, grassy retention area, where water is retained during the monsoon season. The driver-side door flew open, and the drunken boyfriend ran off, straight through the perfectly-groomed grassy area, crossed the street, and headed out of sight, leaving his girlfriend behind. The passenger door opened, her head was down, and I heard her repeated cries:

"I can't believe this!"

"I can't believe he would do this to me."

"He said he loved me."

"Are you ok?" I asked, as I heard my inspired angels' words, "God loves you, trust Him," resonating inside my head.

I could smell spilled beer, as she cried out, "My father is going to kill me!"

"Are you ok?" I asked again.

Gently touching her arm, I said, "Honey, you'll be ok! Honey, do you believe in God?"

I heard her take a deep breath, and with her crying voice, whispered, "Yes."

"Good! God will give you the strength to get through this, and guide you to let go of the boyfriend, who clearly doesn't love you." Holding her in my arms, she began to calm down until the police arrived. Looking over, we watched this tall, large officer walking closer. He had this scowl on his face and walked with authority towards us. I could feel her body shaking as tears flowed down her cheeks. She started to hyperventilate. I gently repeated, "Honey, you'll be ok."

With every breath she could take, she said, "You…you…you don't understand, my…my father is going to kill me!"

I said, "Your father loves you, and God will protect you." The officer walked up and began shouting at her.

"You'll be grounded for months for this!"

I gave her one last hug, whispered, "Stay calm, listen to him, and know God will protect you!" The officer angrily took his daughter home.

Unlike the scorching summer Arizona 110- to 120-degree days, it was a typical beautiful winter Arizona day at 85 degrees. This was the time of year when the neighborhood children came out of their hibernation in their air-conditioned homes to play outside.

While Michelle and Nik played down the street with their friends, I heard a gentle knock on my front door. As I slowly opened the door, this young girl just stared at me through teary eyes and smiled. Her face looked familiar. This time, her tears no longer looked painful, but showed joy and gratitude. She looked up and said, "I have been standing in front of your house for quite some time now, watching you through the window, waiting to see if I should knock or not. I didn't know if you would remember me. I am the girl from the park, whose boyfriend took off and left me to take the heat. You held me, and gave me hope. I came to say thank you! Thank you for caring and changing my life. I was grounded for six months, broke up with my boyfriend, and now have a positive outlook on life."

We hugged and shared our tears of joy. At that moment, I felt like God taught both of us how to let go and trust Him. He is the one who has our life planned out to live for His purpose when we let go and let God.

TROUBLED TEEN—ISOLATED AND ALONE

It was a new day, and the desert wildflowers and beautiful prickly pear cacti were beginning to bloom. Temperatures were still perfect for the children to play outside at the park as the equipment was no longer scorching hot.

"BANG! BANG!"

A loud noise, like a chain hitting metal, came from across the street at the park. He was tall, slim, had a few tattoos and wore baggy jeans and a T-shirt. He was obviously distraught and an angry teenager. He stayed focused, staring at the center of the slide, as he began whipping a huge chain on the slide of the playground equipment. I somehow could feel his pain. Without hesitation, I walked over and calmly said, "I can see you're upset about something, but is it necessary to destroy the children's equipment because of something hurting inside of you?" He didn't say a word, but slowed the aggression of force with each new whip. I then asked him if he would sit with me at the picnic table. The whipping stopped as he stared at the equipment; he contemplated what to do next, sit or just walk away?

I asked him again, "Are you ok? Do you want to talk about it?"

Without looking at me, he pulled the chain closer to his body, turned around, and sat at the picnic table. I asked again, "Honey, would you like to talk about what's upsetting you?" I sat, waited, and listened.

He said, "Why do you care?! All my life, I've been told how 'bad' I am and how no one cares about me, so why do you care?"

I said, "Everything God makes is 'GOOD' and you are no different! God made you and therefore you are good."

He shared his broken stories; we talked about them, and I reiterated what a good person he was. I saw tears filling in his eyes as he stood up. He walked around the table and asked if he could give me a hug.

He said, "No one has ever cared or listened to me like that before. Thank you!"

I said, "God will give you the strength to get through your pain." He left calmly and with a new purpose.

The Lord will guide you always; He will satisfy your needs in a sun-scorched land and will strengthen your frame. You will be like a well-watered garden, like a spring whose waters never fail.

Isaiah 58:11 NIV

TEEN MOB—FAITH OVER FEAR

Several months later, the temps increased and the Arizona summer heat was approaching, but school was not quite out yet. There was a mob of about twenty-five teenagers surrounding one young girl in the park across the street. She clearly cried out, "STOP! LEAVE ME ALONE!" Without hesitation, I walked in the middle of them, and broke up the near fight. While being shouted and cursed at, I ignored the mob and walked up to the little girl. Our eyes connected, and tears fell down her face. I was grateful God put me in her life to save her from that mob. This caused a flashback reminding me of the girl who saved me from the mean girls who wanted to beat me up, and how Ellen was there for me when I was a teenager. But one of the girls in the mob wasn't so grateful. She insisted on screaming and cursing at me, apparently this situation didn't end the way she had hoped. I told her I was going to follow her home so I could meet her parents and confirm they really didn't raise a young girl with such a foul mouth. The longer I followed her the more upset she became. She walked in circles as she knew her parents would not appreciate her disrespectful behavior and nasty language. I then told her I would pray for her and her hidden pain. We went our separate ways.

When one door closes another one opens. God blesses and strengthens us through someone's words and/or actions and gives us hope and encouragement to continue moving forward.

Let no corrupting talk come out of your mouths, but only such as is good for building up, as fits the occasion, that it may give grace to those who hear. Ephesians 4:29 ESV

GOOD SAMARITAN ANGELS

As I continued to move forward along life's journey, each day brought another opportunity to help someone in need. I put my life in God's hands and continued to serve Him. I was the PTO's, Good Samaritan Committee Chair, for the elementary school my children attended. The committee collected money and food for families in need throughout our own community. Michelle, Nik, and I would deliver the collected items to families. We couldn't believe the generosity when the back of my Jeep was fully packed, as we headed out. The children never complained or asked why we were doing the things we did, they were always grateful to be helping others. It was our journey to serve others together and put everything in God's hands.

It was our last stop of the day. As we drove across town, I wondered why we drove so far away from the school, our own community. I never questioned where we had to drive or anything about the families. It was all confidential. If they wanted me to know, they would have told me. We finally reached the apartment complex, and, carrying as many bags as we could, walked up to the door and knocked. As the door opened, we were greeted by a grateful smile from the mom, and my daughter stopped in her tracks and looked like she had just seen a ghost. She stood shocked and just stared into the apartment as though her mind was racing what to do next. I looked at her to see what she was looking at. She stared straight into the living room at a young boy sitting on a broken couch as he slowly looked up at her. No words were spoken as their eyes locked. In that quick second, everything she had witnessed and learned in her life came to fruition. Michelle and Nik were about to get a real understanding of discretion and confidentiality. He looked sad until she smiled and said, "Hi." No other words were spoken but they clearly shared a mutual appreciation.

Our walk back to the Jeep was quiet. Once the jeep doors closed, she began to cry. I asked her what made her so sad, and she said, "That boy is in my class, Mommy! Why did he live so far away? Why don't they have food? Why was his couch broken?" So many questions, yet so much to learn. It reminded me of the in-depth conversation with the fifth-grade religious education class "No one is Homeless this Thanksgiving" newspaper project, years ago. These experiences spark the best conversations.

I explained, "Do you remember when I talked about discretion, confidentiality and how to never judge anyone?"

"Yes," she quietly responded.

"Everyone has a different life story because God made each of us different; it isn't up to us to ask or judge someone because their situation is different than ours. You did the right thing by smiling and saying 'Hi' and not making him feel bad. That's what 'unconditional' means!" I added.

In her mind, she thought everyone lived the same way. I explained, "God gives us these opportunities to be His angels and help others."

Everyone's normal and comfortable lifestyle is his/her "normal." We are not here to judge. Whether you're homeless, live in a big house, an apartment, cook every meal, or go out to restaurants, clean your home, or have a maid, it doesn't matter. We are not here to judge. Only God judges. Judging others leads to misconceptions.

Do not judge, or you too will be judged. Matthew 7:1 NIV

IT'S A MATCH

My love and compassion to help others was evident to my Pastor friend and neighbor. He and his wife, witnessed the love and compassion I had, and asked if I would be interested in mentoring.

I felt honored to be called to the ministry of being a mentor through a Christian organization called MatchPoint. Each Mentor was required to apply, have a background check, and if approved, assigned a case manager; not only for everyone's safety but to find that perfect mentor/mentee connection.

Although the sun was scorching hot, well over 100-degrees in Arizona, where you could fry an egg on the cement in seconds, my life was beaming like sunrays from Heaven. No comforting air-conditioned home was better than what I was about to experience. My case manager picked me up, and we drove across town to meet my MATCH. We drove into an older run down trailer park with each home close to the other, similar to the closeness at the house I grew up in when I was a child, except these were trailer homes, not houses. No sense of privacy. I initially felt sad yet peaceful. I had so much, even an air-conditioned home on this hot day, and these families were trying everything to survive the unbearable heat. As we approached the door, we were instantly greeted with a warmhearted genuine smile from a mom holding a little baby boy, full of life, yet too young to walk. We sat at the small square kitchen table, getting to know one another, waiting for my possible mentee to come home from her friend's house. The door opened and immediately our eyes connected. You could tell she was her mother's daughter as they shared the same warm smile. It was an instant connection. She was so excited; she grabbed my hand and lead me down the narrow hallway towards her bedroom. It was a very small room. She enthusiastically pointed out each of her cherished collectable items. Then, excitedly said, "This is where I sleep." Her bed was a small mattress on the floor. This was her life, and all she knew. We then went for a short walk outside, talking, sharing and briefly getting to know each other. I asked her if she would be ok if I was her mentor. Her smile grew bigger than the initial one when we first met. I teased and said, "By the size of that smile on your face, I would say that was a big 'YES!'"

We began our two-year commitment and a new chapter in our lives. My mentee was a very thin eight-year-old, the same age as my son. She had long sandy blonde hair, and was just as beautiful on the inside as she was on the outside. She had three siblings, two of which were also in the program.

The mentor guidelines stated that we needed to establish a relationship for three months before introducing her to my family. Once a month we participated in a MatchPoint group activity and met weekly doing different activities (going to parks, talking, drawing pictures of things she liked and/or wanted her world to be like; having ice cream; or sharing lunch at her favorite place, Sonic). She always ordered the same thing, a foot-long chili dog and tater tots. I initially thought, "WOW, how does such a little girl eat so much!" Then, each time, she would only eat half of her meal and wrapped up the rest. When I asked her why, she said she wanted to share with her little brother. I admired her tenacity for her family. In my experience, people who had little to none, shared more with others, than people with plenty.

After three months, she finally met my family. They welcomed her with open arms and connected like they were related and in each other's lives since birth. Once in a while, my own children would participate with my mentee and me through her MatchPoint activities. It was a match made in heaven for all of us.

Time together flew by so fast that before we knew it, our "contracted time" ended. We kept in touch and continued to see each other on occasion, which was no longer through MatchPoint, but agreed upon between her mom and me.

God continually used me to plant seeds for my children. They witnessed and learned how, as God's children, we should treat each other, love unconditionally without judgment, and how no one is better than another, no matter what they had, how they lived, or what they did.

ANGELS

I heard throughout my life, "some people aren't meant to be together." How could that refer to me and my husband of over fifteen years. We have children. That quote came to mind when our differences were too different, and the counselors gave it their best. My loneliness and emptiness left my husband and I on opposite pages, and those differences led to divorce proceedings. He moved out, and we agreed it was best for me to stay in the house with the children. My life started over as a single mom. What would I do for a job? It's been too many years out of the corporate world. Who would hire me? So many questions raced through my head, like a roulette wheel, waiting to land on a lucky number…7 maybe? I went to a job agency and took whatever test they gave me to see what my job skills were. The rest was in God's hands.

I needed hope and an angel! My life was changing again!

Where is my angel?

Lord, please send me an angel.

I want to remain a stay-at-home mom and help out at the school!

I'm scared! I feel alone and afraid…going through this divorce.

Lord, you blessed me with these children to take care of, and now who can I trust to watch over my children, especially with family so far away?

The phone rang and the voice on the other end exclaimed, "YOU GOT THE JOB!" Not just a job, but the administrative assistant one at a large pharmaceutical company."

I felt numb and not as excited as I should have been.

I politely asked her, "Thank you. When do I start?"

I hope and pray they understand when I tell them my mom and step-dad are taking the kids and I on vacation to Mexico in two weeks.

"When can you start?" she asked.

"I have a vacation already scheduled, so I could come in for a week and work, but then I would be gone for a week on vacation with my children and parents."

"That would work for us as your new boss is out of town and returns that same day you would be back."

Once the formalities were done, it hit me, *what about the children? Who would watch them?*

I needed to trust God. Kneeling next to my bed, tears flowing, I pleaded and prayed for help. The telephone rang again, and my new neighbor said, "The Holy Spirit guided me to call you. Are you ok?"

I sobbed. She was my angel. God answered my plea and showed me, once again, TRUST in HIM! My angel watched the children and refused to take any money. I knew they were safe and in God's hands.

I repeatedly told myself, *Mary, God's got this! Keep your head up, smile, and walk with confidence.* Believing and trusting God, I confidently started each day walking through the door of opportunity, believing God had a purpose and plan for me. I was where I was supposed to be.

Every day, no matter what was going on or how I felt, I tried my best to start the same way…head up, smiling, and walking with confidence. Believing and trusting God, I confidently started each day walking through the door of opportunity, believing God had a purpose and plan for me. I was where I was supposed to be. And, my boss, Diana, and I were meant to work together. Some may call it a coincidence, I call it all part of God's planning. During my first week on the job, I found out Diana was from Wisconsin. While I was on vacation with my children, mom, and step-dad in Mexico, Diana was on her vacation visiting Wisconsin, and we both started back on the same day.

This day was no different than any other day for the past six months. I walked through the office, passing one department after another, when a co-worker stopped me and said, "May I ask you something?"

"Of course," I replied.

"I watch you every day, and you walk with such confidence, and you're always smiling, so I have to ask, do you EVER have a bad day?"

WOW! Me? Walk with such confidence? You have no idea how heavy my daily cross is. I leave my children with a friend or drop them off at the Boys and Girls Club, while I provide for our newly-broken family. You have no idea how hard I cry myself to sleep at night, after reading bedtime stories, praying, and tucking my children in their beds, as I try to figure out how to be a single parent and handle what will happen next!

"Thank you for noticing, but yes, I do have bad days," I said.

This man saw a grateful woman, blessed to be given such a remarkable job, good pay, great benefits; and a mom who wanted to show her children that, although I could no longer be a "stay-at-home" mom, I could still be the best mom, provider, and caretaker, when we were together.

Although my precious babies were only in elementary school at the time, they were strong and resilient beyond their years. The early mornings were like clockwork. Everyone had their own job to do and the three of us were out the door by 6:30 a.m. without complaints. We not only started our day with me reading the "Daily Word" (a subscription gift given to me when we lived in Michigan by an angel friend, that I renew every year) but started our mornings with the same prayer, "The Promise Prayer," the prayer we learned from the parochial school my daughter, Michelle attended in Michigan. As we got settled in the car, our routine continued with me putting my left hand on the steering wheel and my right on the center console. I felt the first little hand on top of mine and then the weight of the other making us one, as we began in unison saying:

"I Promise Dear Jesus, to follow you today,

to obey your every rule in all I do and say;

to always be a loving child, helpful, kind, and good,

to give the love you give to me to everyone I should

but if this promise I shall break or if I bring you sorrow

then help me to begin again and keep my promise tomorrow."

Even if the morning didn't seem perfect, it was perfect in my eyes starting each day with "The Promise Prayer" and always an "I love you, have a great day," before the car door shut and we departed, going our separate ways for the day.

While I knew life's changes were inevitable, my life was changing faster than I thought I would be ready for. I knew to head to the one place that would give me answers, a message, or even a sign. That one place for me was church, to listen to the teacher, to hear a parable, lesson, or whatever message I needed at the time. While I thought my personal life was the only thing changing, I was dead wrong.

Life was about to change for the worse, so others thought. Life might revert back to living like the olden days without electricity, heat, or running water. The new millennium was arriving, and the fear of the unknown was getting to people. Desperate times lead to desperate measures. Some people actually thought the world was going to end.

Whenever I felt scattered or scared, not only did praying and listening to Christian music help but attending church services always brought me back to reality and centered me to feel at peace about whatever I was going through in life. This particular Sunday, when I arrived, the church was packed…standing room only. At the end of the aisle I could hear, "Everyone please move closer, so we can have more people seated!" Under normal circumstances, we might have felt that squeezed-in-like-sardines-feeling and very uncomfortable, but this was different. It was almost as if the closer we were to each other, the more comforting it became. We were all connected as one family in this big universe. Although we were all believers, desperate times were the times to hear messages from the teacher, His parable lessons, and to help us understand what we were going through. While waiting for the service to begin, I looked around at the crowd and reflected on how grateful I was for the opportunity to have a wonderful corporate job, especially as a single mom. Suddenly, I was startled by a gentle touch on my right leg. I quickly turned my head and saw the gentlest smile and a look of mixed emotions. Was she trying to tell me something? Was she scared? It was as if we were all there for the same reason. We were coming together as a community, a church, and one nation under God. This gently smiling elderly woman leaned towards me and whispered, "I bet you're a wonderful teacher."

I wish I was a teacher.

I said, "I would love to be a teacher."

Again, she leaned in and said, "You're a great teacher and students love you!" Her eyes sparkled, her face lit up, and a lifetime of stories I was sure could be told by the many wrinkles across her face. It was as though we were connected in a different way, at some deeper level, and I longed to sit down with her and hear all about those life stories.

I smiled and quietly said, "Thank you, but I'm not a teacher."

How does she know what I really wanted to do? She was definitely adamant about me being a teacher. It was something I could never do as a single mom…leave my great paying job with a large pharmaceutical company and great benefits.

I couldn't stop thinking about it. As we walked up to receive Holy Communion I turned to sit back down, and she was gone. Gone so fast my head spun in every direction trying to find her. I couldn't see her walking away in any direction. She was right there next to me. How could she be gone so quickly? I know the church was packed, but she was old and frail looking; there was no way she could have ran out of church that fast. So many questions were racing in my head, as I no longer could focus on anything except looking around the entire church hoping I would see her. Generally, people, especially the older generation, never left the church early like that.

Why did she tell me I was a teacher?

What just happened?

She was right next to me and real! I felt her touch. How could she disappear and walk away so fast?

She planted a seed. From that day forward, I questioned what I was doing with my life. Was I really happy being an administrative assistant in the big corporate world?

Reflecting back on my days in Jackson, Michigan, I was often told by friends and neighbors I would make a good teacher. Just like the woman I met on the golf course offered me the opportunity to team-teach the religious education class. And the fact that I was already a "structured mom" made me feel like a teacher with my own children. I loved teaching them new things, encouraging them to use their imagination and to never stop dreaming. Our weekly routine consisted of making breakfast together, having a morning activity at 10:00 (making a craft, going for a walk and to the library, playing in the sandbox, going to the park, making cookies, or pulling out the "Dress Up Box" so they could use their imagination with the box of old clothes, shoes, and jewelry), lunch at noon, story time afterwards, naptime, an afternoon activity, and then, while I made dinner, the children would pretend to cook with their bowl of flour and water. There was very little TV time.

To my surprise, a co-worker at the pharmaceutical company asked if I wanted to take night classes with her. The company encouraged furthering education anyway, so this was perfect. I thought, maybe someday my dream to be a teacher would come true. I stayed up late after the children went to bed, completed homework, wrote papers, or researched. I didn't realize how hard I was working until I received an invitation to an induction into a Phi Theta Kappa ceremony, sponsored by my English teacher. She was the engaging type of teacher I wanted to be. It didn't matter the age of the students in her class, whether 18 or 80. Yes, I said 80. There was an 80-year-old taking classes because she loved to learn. She was my inspiration.

Fortunately, or unfortunately I was adjusting to my life as a single mom. Then I received a call I never thought I would get. The divorce wasn't final; the papers were never finalized by the court and somehow got "lost in the mail." Now what? Was it fate? Were we not to divorce? I put the decision in God's hands and just let things happen. My husband and I began to talk, date, and let go and let God. I continued my schooling while working at the pharmaceutical company in Scottsdale, Arizona.

While continuing night classes and another year as an administrative assistant passed, I received a call from my friend, Lorene Eisenhauer, who at one time was my son's preschool teacher. Lorene said there was a new charter school opening across the street from the elementary school my children attended, and they were looking for a Pre-K teacher. She continued, "I know you have a job, but I think you would be perfect for this job. We could work together and team-teach. Think about it, and get back to me." Team teach? That sounded familiar!

I thought, an interview couldn't hurt, RIGHT?!

I agreed to go for the interview and had a very important decision to make. I made my pros and cons list: a huge pay cut, less benefits, but closer to home, more time with my children, AND fulfilling a dream I thought would never come true.

While I prayed to make the right decision, the light bulb went on, my heart was filled, and the Holy Spirit was getting my attention, LOUD and clear! I remembered the elderly woman at church before the new millennium, who told me I was a teacher, and the 80-year-old in class, who told everyone, "You're never too old to make dreams come true." There was my sign. I went in and talked to my boss and told her about my difficult decision. Diana's best advice was, "Never live with regrets." She added, "If you didn't take the teaching job, would you be ok with your decision staying here, setting aside the money and benefits?" Although she didn't want to lose me, she said she didn't want to hold me back from fulfilling a dream. She taught me many lessons, professionally and personally. The calm feeling inside confirmed I needed to take a leap of faith and walk away from the corporate high-paying, great-benefits job, to be a Pre-K teacher. It was a dream come true. While my corporate world door closed and I mentally prepared myself for the next chapter of my life, my thoughts were like a meteor shower inside my head, a beautiful sight to see, but shooting from all directions.

I was startled when my cell phone rang and it was my friend Lorene, who needed my help. There was a parent meeting at the charter school, and she had a family emergency. She would be there at the beginning of the meeting and help me get started but couldn't stay the entire time. I replayed what I would say to the parents over and over inside my head as I continued to drive from my last day at the corporate job to what would be my new job.

It doesn't matter that I hadn't started my new job as a teacher yet, RIGHT? And, I didn't know what I didn't know; nor what to expect or was required of me. I could do this. You've got this Mary! Let go and let God. You took a leap of faith for a reason!

I walked into what was going to be my new classroom, filled with parents. Lorene gave a quick introduction and then said she needed to leave for a family emergency but they were in good hands with me. Under normal circumstances I would have stood there frozen or speechless, or furious, and scared to death, but I was actually calm. I was doing what I was called to do…be a Teacher and make a difference.

My days never felt like work. I loved teaching, and going to work was a gift. I was making a difference and teaching those little ones with their sponge-like minds soaking up every lesson plan.

They learned and recited weekly poems and history projects, sang songs and played musical instruments, learned colors and counted to 10 in both French and Spanish, had one-on-one writing, coloring, cut and paste time, and a group sensory, craft, and puzzle center.

Teaching wasn't a job; it was a way of life for me. It was what I had already been doing in many ways with my own children… telling them, "Every day is a school day." We all learn something new every day, whether in school or not. And, now, I was sharing the knowledge with my students. The difference I was making in their little lives enhanced my drive to make more of a difference, even stronger.

"To the world you may be one person
but to one person you may be the world."
- Dr. Seuss

While I was just doing what came naturally, to my surprise, my good works, words and actions were apparently making a difference and not only in the classroom but outside. Parents would say, "Keep doing what you're doing, because it's making a difference at home, and I hear what you're teaching through my daughter's excitement." I give God all the glory for the difference I was making by sharing the gift of wisdom and knowledge to the students.

So do not fear, for I am with you; do not be dismayed, for I am your God. I will strengthen you and help you; I will uphold you with my righteous right hand. Isaiah 41:10 NIV

CHAPTER FOUR

WISDOM

An attraction to the divine, acting upon both the intellect and the will

A Calling

For we walk by faith, not by sight.
2 Corinthians 5:7 NKJV

FAITH/FEELING/CALLING

D o you ever feel called to doing something? Called to love, be kind, supportive, compassionate, or serve another?

How are you guided to your calling? Is a travel guide guiding you towards your new destinations? Are you receiving insight, wisdom, or is a feeling directing you? Do you question if this is the right thing to do, place to go, or change to make?

I knew I was being called to do, go, or change something. I answered the call of my heart. When I put tough decisions or self-doubt in God's hands, a feeling of peace and calm came over me.

What should have been an end of a marriage became a calling for reconciliation. This once broken family was together again. Another opportunity arose to move and start over, a fresh new beginning, and a chance to see the "real" Rocky Mountains. I agreed, and off to Colorado we went as a family. Although no longer a pre-school teacher, I was called to be a paraeducator and get involved in the schools. While I held the position of PTO president, which led to great connections, I secured the front office secretary position at a brand-new middle school, Rocky Top. It was as though God gave me yet another message with His great sense of humor, feeling "on TOP of the world" in the heart of the Rocky Mountains. This job was a calling, especially when I heard over 200 people applied, and I was the chosen one. The parents and students were excited to see their new school, and I was excited to begin my new journey.

My calling may not have been to teach in the schools, but God was talking and I was listening. I was also called to be a fifth grade Sunday School teacher, and take Holy Communion to the homebound. These were callings and gifts I respectfully accepted!

The Rocky Mountains were as beautiful as ever. The hot sun shining on the snow-topped mountains gave this Sunday an even more glorious look. Sunday school classes were over, and we were onto our homebound stops before heading home. Most often, the children went with me. Our first stop was an assisted living/ nursing home. Although the large building was three levels, it was easy to get around the square floor plan and the one securely locked area for those who needed special care 24/7. We set up for a mini Mass, while the residents carefully entered the Chapel. Readings were said, Holy Communion was distributed, and then after closing prayers we went to the individual rooms for those who were unable to attend the service. Regardless of their reason for not attending Mass, bringing Holy Communion to them not only lit up their faces but put peace in my heart. They loved the company as much as we loved being there.

Nik, being my youngest, was so inquisitive and asked a lot of questions, "Why do they get so excited to see us, Momma? Don't they have a family?"

"Not everyone is called to serve others like we are. It's our gift to them," I explained.

"Well, I'm glad we can do this and bring them smiles, Mommy!" he happily said.

I was so proud of my children for never complaining they had to go to these homes with me. They never felt obligated; it was just what we did every Sunday.

We headed to our last home for the day, a ranch home in a neighborhood. The nurse on call opened the door, and as we walked in she introduced us to each guests, whether we were there specifically to give them Holy Communion or not. As we walked in, the kitchen was straight in front of us with a family room nearby, and immediately to our right was a quaint living room area. There were bedrooms on both sides of the house. The right side was for the assisted living guests, and on the left were the hospital rooms that housed the more fragile guests. Off the kitchen was a patio and small fenced-in yard with chairs strategically placed for a quieter meditative-like setting. There were usually four to six guests and a constant rotating shift of nurses as well as the owners who were also in the medical field. Everyone was a gift in his or her own way. It was definitely their calling to serve others.

While only two of the guests were Catholic, who we prayed with and gave Holy Communion to, we found ourselves connecting with all the guests, which were all women except for one man named Bobby. Bobby sat in a chair in the family room and never said a word. He would just stare out the window. As my daughter Michelle and I were talking to the other women, my son Nik, curiously or courageously, walked up to Bobby and said, "Hello." Bobby's nonresponsive words or actions did not stop Nik. He was persistent in sharing his gift of communication. He began talking to Bobby as though they were having a conversation back and forth, but Nik was the only one talking. While building relationships week after week, I think we learned more about each other than we ever imagined. One woman, from Panama, would cry as she shared how she felt her children left her behind. I thought at first maybe she was suffering Alzheimer's and couldn't remember if they were there or not, but the nurses confirmed her family hadn't been there in over a year. There was apparently one excuse after another keeping the families away. I've heard stories of families putting their parents in a home while they get on with their lives, but this was my first time witnessing the pain on the face of a broken parent. She obviously brought them into this world, and I'm sure she was there when they needed her while growing up. It made me so sad. It was definitely our calling to be there and be their extended family. We said our goodbyes but promised to be back the next week.

Sunday came again, and it was another beautiful sunny day in Colorado as we headed back to the nursing home to visit our extended families. The ladies were in their same chairs and so was Bobby. This time, Nik brought a small ball. He walked straight up to Bobby, like he always did, greeted him with his big smile and his loving heart, then gently rolled the ball by Bobby's feet. We were startled, when all of a sudden Bobby made this loud noise and wouldn't stop. Nik was scared and the nurse came running with excitement. We were all confused for a moment. She said, that noise is his way of expressing excitement.

"He is happy, Nik. He loves playing ball with you," the nurse said.

It made me cry tears of joy. This little blessing of mine, never gave up on Bobby, even when he wouldn't respond, and continued to build a relationship with him.

We all watched as Nik walked back up to him and rolled the ball towards his feet. Bobby gently kicked the ball back. It was their new game. Because of our trusted friendship with Bobby, he allowed us to give him a hug, and by the time we left, tears were running down his cheeks. Nik gave him another hug and excitedly said, "I'll see you next week."

The next week came, and when we walked into the house, Bobby wasn't in the chair. Nik quickly turned toward me, tears filled his eyes with a sense of a loss, when suddenly the patio door opened and the nurse came in from outside. She said, "Bobby is waiting outside for you, Nik and Michelle! You all have been angels to Bobby; he hasn't communicated or made any sounds in years, after his abuse by caretakers at a previous home. You brought life back to him! Outside, there were two chairs set up and a larger ball by Bobby. Bobby stood this time, in front of the chair, and tossed the ball to Nik while making the loudest excited noises I had ever heard. This was a gift for all of us.

While Nik and Michelle were out in the yard keeping Bobby company, one of the nurses asked me to come back into the house with her. We walked to the left side of the house, the side where the more fragile guests lived.

She said, "There is someone I would like you to meet. She is not Catholic, but she is not doing well and needs prayers." As we walked into the room, there, in a hospital bed, lay an elderly woman attached to many monitors. I reached over and held her hand. I asked the Holy Spirit to help me speak the right words and lift her up to the Lord. While the nurse stood next to the woman on the opposite side of me, I said whatever the good Lord wanted me to say at that time. This woman was unable to speak but I knew she could hear the prayer when I saw tears running down the side of her face. I told her she was in God's hands. The nurse thanked me, as she didn't think this woman would make it through the night. She passed away that afternoon.

Months later, when we walked in, Bobby wasn't sitting in his chair inside or outside. He had gotten sick and ended up in the hospital. He never returned to the home. We were grateful for the opportunity to embrace our calling and our differences, and to share our God-given gifts—the gifts of unconditional love and compassion.

OUR GIFT

Although my Arizona mentee was a gift to me and my family at the time, her mother needed to know what a gift she was to her own daughter. I was shocked by the call I received while living in Colorado from my Arizona mentee's mom, asking if her daughter could come live with us, or if we could possibly even adopt her.

"She would have a 'better' life with you," said her mother.

I told her, "You are the best gift you can give her, just love her unconditionally!" It was an opportunity to mentor my mentee's mom on how God made us different for His purpose, and we all have gifts to share.

"Take all the lessons learned and continue being the great mom that you are! You gave your children an opportunity to be part of such a wonderful organization. You don't need 'things' to love your children unconditionally," I reminded her.

We are all different and everything happens for a reason and in God's timing and for His purpose. We are not here to judge nor compare. We all have a purpose.

It was God's Will, a calling to share what a gift the mentee's mom was to her own children.

Therefore I tell you, do not worry about your life, what you will eat or drink; or about your body, what you will wear. Is not life more than food, and the body more than clothes? Matthew 6:25 NIV

CHAPTER FIVE

COUNSEL

*Operate under the guidance of the Holy Spirit
to illuminate the will of God*

Differences

*Do not judge, or you too will be judged.
For in the same way you judge others, you
will be judged, and with the measure you
use, it will be measured to you.*

Matthew 7:1-2 NIV

DON'T JUDGE A BOOK BY ITS COVER

Let's Face it. We are all different. God made us that way for a reason. It's better to embrace our differences than to criticize.

Once again, my husband and I tried to embrace our real differences even through attending marriage counseling, but ultimately, we decided it was best to go our separate ways. I was a single mom once again. There was comfort in knowing I had a job at the middle school, but extra money would give relief, and the school administrators offered me an opportunity to work part-time as a custodian on Sundays.

It was quiet and actually peaceful…a "silence is golden" kind of moment…as I walked down the dark, lonely hallways, turning one light on at a time and unlocking doors. As I finished setting up one of the rooms, I heard sounds I had never heard during the school week coming from the vents. I ignored the creepy vent noises and headed down the hall, opened a closet door, and got out my supplies, when the silence began to dissipate. I walked towards the cafeteria and greeted the people I passed as they headed into the sanctuary and began their church service celebration. While leaning against the lockers, listening from afar, I closed my eyes and took in the beautiful sound of Christian music. I was in awe. It was a temporary mindful vacation away from the internal pain of my new divorce journey.

I had all but two bathrooms outside the cafeteria left to clean. As the church service ended, I stood to the side, holding the handle of the mop, when this beautiful, nicely dressed woman walked up to me. I smiled and she looked straight into my eyes, with a stern look, and said, "Excuse me but you missed a spot!" while pointing to the floor. She turned and abruptly stomped away.

WOW! That did not just happen to me, I thought. *Did you not just get out of your church service? Or, is this a facade, thinking you're a better Christian woman in a beautiful dress and high heels, than me working on a Sunday, in my blue jeans, T-shirt, and tennis shoes, scrubbing floors and cleaning toilets?*

I stood shocked and dismayed. I pulled out a piece of paper and to my surprise my thoughts turned into a poem I titled, *Differences.* God turned my mess into a message.

Differences

See the differences in you and me
they're really quite simple just look and see;
not just the color of your eyes or hair
or how your skin is dark or fair
not the clothes or how they fit
fully describe your personality or wit.
The way you speak or even smile
does not describe you calm or wild.
The sound of music makes your voice carry.
Their words and songs can make it vary.
God made us each a little unique;
depend on Him when you are weak.
Accept our differences just look and see
They're really quite simple as can be.

— Mary A. Markham

I can't let this bother me. Remember, God turned my Sunday mess into a glorious message. I'm in His hands!

Even though it was a beautiful, warm, and sunny Monday in the Rocky Mountains I needed to wear a light sweater paired with my long skirt and heels as the school air conditioner forced a chill into my office. A new day, a new week, and I was already back in my daily routine…no longer silence! Every time the office door opened, noise erupted in the hallway from parents and students, or echoed from the lockers slamming shut as the students talked and reminisced about their weekends. It was a typical, busy day at the middle school. Having the opportunity to supplement my income as a custodian every other Sunday surely helped this newly divorced middle school secretary.

Busy typing away at the computer, I heard a familiar voice.

"Excuse me!" I looked up, and before I could say a word, this woman said, "Excuse me, I need to drop this"…and before she finished her sentence, she said, "Do I know you? You look so familiar."

I smiled and said, "I'm a secretary by day and a custodian by night." Her face immediately turned red, clearly from embarrassment, remembering how she treated me, as a custodian, the day before, after the church service. She didn't know what to say next. The awkward moment came to an end when I politely asked how I could help her. Too embarrassed, I'm guessing, is why she never apologized, and my politeness was my way of forgiving her.

I would like to think, as she walked away that day, she learned to never judge a book by its cover again.

Do not judge, and you will not be judged. Do not condemn, and you will not be condemned. Forgive, and you will be forgiven. Give, and it will be given to you. A good measure, pressed down, shaken together and running over, will be poured into your lap. For with the measure you use, it will be measured to you. Luke 6:37-38

FLASHBACK

As I read the poem Differences, it reminded me of the time in high school when my mom wanted me to invite my friends over for our traditional Saturday homemade pizza night.

I CAN'T! She's different than us!

"She has it all!" Her mom and dad are still married; they live in a big, fancy, white house, out in the middle of nowhere or it seemed like "in the middle of nowhere" to this city girl. Her beautiful house was set in the country surrounded by God's creations with beautiful flowers blooming on the front and side of the house, and large trees; and I'm sure it was filled with many stories if the walls could talk. There were acres between houses so you couldn't hear your neighbor talking like I could in the city. There was so much space; her yard seemed so huge. I pictured myself running around feeling like I had no care in the world. She had a large bedroom all to herself, and as I walked through her house, I remember thinking how it looked like one of those homes you would see in a magazine, perfectly displayed and with everything matching. I couldn't ever imagine being that rich and having everything she had. She was the luckiest girl in the world, and I wished I had what she had.

Our house was older, a little more run down; I'm sure it could share many stories too if it could talk. We lived in the upper-level of a small duplex in the city. My mom and two of my siblings shared this small three-bedroom, one-bath, apartment style house. The houses were so close together that when the windows were open, you could hear the neighbor's music or television. There was nothing fancy about our house, but it was "home." Our carpet was green, and our furniture didn't match. The furniture was given to us from St. Vincent de Paul. This was my "normal," and the life I knew. Saturday nights were the best. It was homemade pizza night! First, we would make the pizza dough, set that aside to rise, and then cut the veggies. We cooked the sausage, and then whipped up Mom's homemade sauce. My mom was the master. She didn't measure the ingredients, but just added tomato paste, water, garlic, oregano, Italian seasoning, and a little sugar until the taste was to her liking. Sometimes we would make our own individual pizzas or make a few large ones, and all in attendance played a part in the cooking/ making pizza process. It was a favorite time for me!

"Ok…I listened to you, Mom, and trusted God and invited two girlfriends from school over for Saturday night pizza night," I told my mom.

That morning I was so nervous. I was afraid that once they saw where I lived, they would never want to visit again or continue to be my friend. It was dumb. My mom taught me to never judge others, so why was I? As they walked through the front door, I watched them both as they quickly scanned the room; my heart was racing, and then, no judgment, no stares, just a warm smile and a big hello hug! My heart instantly felt at ease, as the smiles turned to laughs, and the laughs turned into nonstop conversations. Their faces lit up when they found out we were making our own pizza from scratch.

They hadn't done that before. We laughed and joked while making the pizzas and sharing dinner together. Having guests over didn't stop our traditions. We paused, thanked the good Lord for our food, as well as the blessing of friendships. It was the best night ever, better than I could have ever dreamed of. Later that week, I went back to my friend's house, the one that looked like it belonged in a beautiful home décor magazine. This time, no longer feeling jealous, we sat on her bed, sharing stories, when I heard her voice crack. I looked up and saw tears in her eyes.

"Did I say something wrong?" I asked.

"No, you are so lucky! You have such a loving family, and I'd give anything to have what you have," she cried.

WOW! She did not just say what I said about her. I told her I wanted what she had. With tears in her eyes, she replied, "No, you don't! My parents never talk; they just argue, otherwise the house is quiet, and we don't eat many meals together, and we certainly don't pray together. I would love to have what you have."

That day changed me. I would never judge or wish to have what someone else had. We all have a story, no matter how big our house is or how much money is in our bank account.

Our differences are what make us beautiful inside and out. Our differences make us unique, gifted, and talented to perform whatever job we are meant for while fulfilling our purpose. Growing up, I remembered hearing, "Only doctors and lawyers make good money and live in big houses." Does that mean, I will never have money or live in a big house? Does it matter if I don't have money and live in a tiny house? Life is what we make it. Comparing takes away our joy and our own abilities. My parents weren't doctors or lawyers, and we once lived in a huge house, at least it was huge to me. In my eyes, my parents were not judgmental people and did all they could to provide for us. Vacations revolved around visiting family, and we drove wherever we went. We never had fancy cars or fancy things. But, who defines fancy? Who defines or decides how to measure how we are supposed to live or how much we are supposed to have? God will provide, no matter how much we make or where we live.

I learned to embrace the differences between us.

END OF FLASHBACK

It was another exciting day at the middle school. Our roles are all unique, but we are there for the same reason—to make a difference!

The students made me smile, and my close co-worker friends filled my emptiness, but it still wasn't the same. My broken heart and broken marriage made me miss my mom even more. What seemed like just another day at the middle school was, unbeknownst to me, a day that would change my life, my future, and my journey. A co-worker, originally from Wisconsin, told me about an airline deal. Perfect, I'll get away from this pain and go spend time with my mom.

God planted the seeds for the next chapter of my life.

The security line seemed forever long, and I thought maybe by the time I got through the long line, some of my pain would dissolve and turn into excitement as I got closer to my Wisconsin destination. The longer I waited at the gate, the more anxious I felt. I even thought it would be best if I didn't talk to anyone, especially men, because of my anger, brokenness, and disappointed emotions. Before boarding the plane, my friend Cathy Church called to wish me well and pray with me. After praying, she said, "Mary, God will bless you with a loving man in your life in His time, not yours." Finally boarding the plane and yet still feeling sad, I couldn't believe how deep the pain really encompassed me. I was glad I had a window seat as I clutched my book, *A Purpose Driven Life,* when a tall, clean-cut man with dark brown hair and a receded hairline, approached my row. I thought to myself, *No way! I am not going to talk to him.* I immediately turned my head, not saying a word, and closed my eyes as I leaned on the window. I heard the pilot's voice over the loud speaker say, "We have reached 30,000 feet."

The man I ignored for the first hour and a half of the flight, asked me what I was reading while he handed me a trail mix bar, which was given out earlier, while I was sleeping…or ignoring him. His gorgeous, hazel, blue eyes and his cutest chin dimple warmed my heart. He shared his story…divorced with two boys. I shared mine…going through a divorce, have a daughter and a son. We shared our faith and longed for the same things.

I said, "We've talked so much, we forgot the obvious, by the way, my name is Mary."

"And mine is Craig," he said, as we both laughed.

I thought, *Really God? What is happening to me? I'm supposed to hate men right now.* He was not only good-looking, had a great smile, but was a Christian too! Many emotions spun in my head. He glanced over, with a smirk, and asked, "Would you ever move back to Wisconsin?"

My quick immediate response was an adamant one, "No! Never! I live in Colorado!"

I thought to myself, *just because you're good-looking, doesn't mean I'm going to move back to Wisconsin.*

Was I really ignoring that still small voice, *Trust Me!* How was I trusting God when all I was thinking about were reasons I wouldn't move back to Wisconsin?

Our nonstop conversation led to the exchange of telephone numbers and email addresses. Craig reached into his wallet, pulled out a business card (clearly not a normal practice…giving out business cards on an airplane), as I smiled watching his hand shake trying to write his phone number and personal email address on the card. He was so cute and the butterflies in my stomach made me feel like a teenager. My sadness turned to joy, and I felt a little more skip to my step, and I felt the biggest smile on my face, as I walked down the jet way, wondering *what just took place?* It was the complete opposite of how this trip started. I wondered, *would I ever really see him again?*

While getting ready for the day, my mind replayed over and over this movie-like love-at-first-sight experience. I couldn't stop thinking of how connected I felt to this stranger I met 30,000 feet in the air…how nice he was…how alike we were in many ways…sharing our beliefs and our easy conversation. I had been praying, and I put my life in God's hands, so this must be fate. I wondered, *did he feel the same way? How could I find out if he felt the same way without being too obvious or pushy? I know! I'll text him and just say something nice. He won't reply, I'm sure he's too busy and certainly not thinking about me.* I picked up my flip phone and texted, "It was really nice meeting you! Thank you for a great conversation!" I put my phone down and finished getting ready and within seconds, he responded. We both couldn't believe the connection. I wanted to hear his voice again, so I called. We chatted for a while and the butterflies continued fluttering when he said he couldn't let me leave without saying goodbye.

Before heading through security on my way back to Colorado, I saw this tall good-looking man, walking with authority, a skip in his step so to speak, with a smile from ear to ear coming towards me. He wrapped his arms around me, picked me right up off the ground, and gave me the biggest hug. He was my gentle giant, my knight in shining armor, and we definitely felt the same way about each other. It was a bittersweet trip; I left my family, this incredibly nice guy I just met, and I headed back to be with my precious babies, who I adored and loved more than anything.

At the time, I enjoyed working at the middle school, even with the office cattiness. I knew there was only one way to get my answers, put this in God's hands. I would go back to my apartment, every day, at lunch, get on my knees and pray. I would say, "God, if this is something you want me to do, I need answers…I need a real sign."

We prayed as a family and conversations with the kids were open and honest. They were adaptable because of the many moves they endured already in their little lives. They weren't afraid of making new friends in a new place, like I was at their age. Still, I couldn't take them away from my ex-husband. Wisconsin would never happen.

"You have more family here than Colorado," Craig reminded me.

This ended up being the clincher for my ex-husband. He realized the children would get to know all of their grandparents in Wisconsin…his parents too. He granted me the right to move the kids out of state. God had taken down all the barriers, and He grew discontentment in me for my work environment. He reminded me of my adaptable children and opened the path for them to move across the country.

We continued to pray as a family and kept the move to ourselves until we knew that it was going to happen. Craig and I talked for endless hours on the telephone while getting to know each other. I believe the longest conversation was a straight five hours. We definitely wanted to make sure this was a good move for everyone. The long distance became too difficult to bear so we decided to take turns traveling back and forth every few months. It was an opportunity to get to know each other and our families better. It was a costly long distant relationship, but after a year of this back and forth game that we no longer wanted to play, we put our relationship in God's hands, and everything fell into place. God led Craig and Nik in a Penske truck, and Michelle and I in our loaded car, safely to Wisconsin. During the drive from Colorado to Wisconsin, Craig had to listen to an audio book for work…*Good to Great.* Little did he know how fitting that was! God blended our two families and four children better than many blood-related siblings bond.

Craig, Mitchell, and Austin got Michelle, Nik, me moved into our new home. We lived seven minutes apart. Our blended family wove together like a beautiful tapestry. Unlike when I grew up being the only girl, and the youngest with three older brothers, Michelle was the oldest and the only girl. Craig's oldest son Mitchell was next in the age bracket, then my son Nik, and then Craig's youngest, Austin. Craig and I blended our beliefs, traditions, and discipline as best as we could. It was not only a match made in heaven between Craig and I, but Michelle, Mitchell, Nik and Austin were always happy for the other, embraced their differences, and cheered each other on in whatever activity or life-path they took.

Although my children were used to living in homes where the houses were right next door and in neighborhoods with sidewalks and cul de sacs to play in, we moved to a place, as my son had said, in the "middle of nowhere." But it is somewhere. We moved to a home not a house, a beautiful and safe place full of unconditional love surrounded by God's creations, and a place filled with a lifetime of great memories. Memories of sharing every meal together and praying before those meals, going to church as a family, conversations lasting hours after meals completed, and a heartfelt love and laughter whenever our blended family got together. This is a place our blended family calls home.

Our family

Craig and I have been married since 2012, and we are now empty nesters. I may not be washing or shaving my his face yet, but when I look at my husband, my smile reminds me of the same smile I saw on my grandmother's face, when she looked at my grandpa. Craig and I joke that our unconditional marriage will only last until I'm 99, then all bets are off! Or, as long as the good Lord decides. I'm hoping to break 100!

Repeatedly hearing, *Trust God*. I questioned if there was a bigger reason why everything fell into place?

Finally, I had more one-on-one time with Mom. It was a sunny, crisp September day; she insisted on picking me up for lunch. Looking at her as I climbed into the car, I blurted, "WOW Mom, you look absolutely beautiful! What did you do different? You look like an angel!" She was glowing, beautiful as ever; but that day seemed different. We ordered food off the menu neither one of us should have been eating. Mom said, "You only live once...let's do it!" Calamari and deep fried onion rings started our healthy lunch. We laughed, cried, and reminisced about life. Gently reaching over, she grabbed my hands, looked straight into my eyes, and said things about my life, future, and people leaving me, and although I would be alone, not to be scared. She said, "God gave me strength, and now I am giving you all my strength."

"Mom, you're scaring me." I said. She took both her hands, placed them on my face, and said, "I love you and give you all my strength." Then she kissed me on the lips, which was something she never did before.

The following week, she wasn't feeling well. Our year of new memories and unforgettable lunches turned into a nightmare.

Whooping and hollering for our favorite football team to score, whistles and cheers were no longer heard after answering my telephone. The words haunted me, "Mom has pancreatic cancer." Tears flowing, I felt sick and motionless.

I can't lose my mom. NO! Not now! Not EVER!

I just moved back, and we're closer than ever. What about the kids? Their grandmother!

Oh…my head spun. *Was THIS the reason God made everything happen and moved me back to Wisconsin? Is that why my co-worker told me about the flight? Is that why Craig was on that plane sitting next to me?* Our future trips and dreams were gone, forever. I felt sad, angry, devastated, and alone. *Wait!* I thought, *alone, is that why she told me I would be alone?* She warned me. Everything said at lunch that day was coming true.

GOD PREPARED HER TO PREPARE ME

Four months later, my mom passed away. Many times, during my life I heard people say, "If I only had one more day with…(fill in the blank), I would…(fill in the blank)." That was me those last four months. I tried to ask every question I could think of; I tried to spend as much time as I could while I was working full time and still providing for my own children. Our extended families tried to spend quality time with Mom as much as possible as well. Although my mom's awareness and energy level were decreasing, and her taste buds changed from all the medication and cancer running through her body, we still managed to set up "family homemade pizza night." The unforgettable smile on my mom's face will last a lifetime. She was so happy with whomever could make it as she carried on our family tradition; she made the dough from scratch as everyone had a different role, cutting up fresh vegetables, making homemade pizza sauce, cooking the Italian sausage, and making sure everyone had their favorite beverage. It was tradition to open a bottle of wine and toast to all of us being together. Mom asked for a small glass of cheer, but her taste buds no longer enjoyed the taste of wine; however, her smile remained as big as ever. As the afternoon went on, I saw that curious look in her eyes, as though she was soaking up every memory she could take with her.

It was getting colder, and an ice storm had begun when I received a call in the middle of the night from my mom requesting my immediate presence. I left a note on the table for the children in case they woke up, called Craig to tell him where I was going, and just left. I didn't talk to anyone on my way, except God. I prayed the entire drive to her house, which was about 20 minutes on a normal day, but took me about 45 minutes because of the icy roads. When I ran into the house, there stood my siblings and a few spouses.

"What is going on? Did something happen?" I asked frantically.

My mom looked at me and asked me to come over by her. She grabbed my hand and said, "I called each of you here; Mary, I want you to give me my last rites."

"Mom, I'm not a minister," I told her.

Again, she repeated, "Mary, I asked all of you here and want you to give me my last rites." When my mom told me something, I knew better than to ever disobey her. I allowed the Holy Spirit to give me the words and blessing over my mother, and finished the prayer holding each other's hands as we recited "The Lord's Prayer" together.

On February 13, 2008, while working at a law firm, I was called to the front reception desk. I received two boxes of roses. I immediately went back to my desk and called Craig and said, "You better not have spent all that money and bought me two dozen roses!"

"I didn't, Honey," he said. "I ordered one dozen for Valentine's Day," he continued.

There I stood, dead in my tracks and began to cry. I said, "Today is the day. My mom is dying today, and this was her way of saying goodbye."

I did what I knew would make my mom happy…I shared a rose with every woman in the office. Before leaving work, I took one dozen and walked from one end of the law office to the other, and said, "This is a gift from my mom." I then left work and drove to her house. Michelle was able to drive, so she and Nik met me at Grandma's house. The three of us held her hand, prayed together, and just talked to her. I thanked her for the beautiful roses as we watched a tear fall from the corner of her eye. My mom knew about a personal appointment I had, and I knew better than to cancel it. I told her I would be right back, and that we loved her very much. My stepdad told me she

took her last breath just before I pulled into the driveway. I believe she did not want me to witness her last breath. I held her in my arms as long as I could that night. My best friend, my mother, and my children's grandmother was gone forever. The children had divorced parents, lived in a new state, and now had lost their grandmother; I worried about them. An image of Ellen handing me her cherished Bible flashed through my head. Was I trusting and listening to the still small voice, *Let Go Let God?*

I needed to let go and let God by living and sharing my faith, just like I witnessed Ellen do. While witnessing my stepdad still very distraught, losing his wife of twenty-seven years, I continued to encourage him. As he witnessed the changes in my life, he wanted to experience the same.

FORGIVING A LIVING NIGHTMARE

Was he lonely or just keeping a dark secret? There was nothing extraordinary about this Saturday when I found, in the mailbox, a sealed envelope with no stamp or return address, just "Mary" handwritten in the center of envelope. I walked curiously into the house, as I began to open this mysterious envelope. As I read the letter, I stood shocked and motionless; my chest felt tight while my heart pounded heavily. I felt anger inside and out. The open windows on that hot summer night kept me from screaming at the top of my lungs. *What was he thinking? He must be confused and distraught over Mom's death,* I thought. While trying to process what was happening, I opened my email and became even more shocked. *How could this man, who was like a father to me, whom I trusted, write such shocking letters and emails expressing his love for me?* Then the stalking began. It felt like everywhere I turned I saw him watching me. This was a living nightmare, the kind you wake up screaming, "NO! STOP!" and no one hears you. **I trusted God**, and He gave me strength to end all ties with my stepdad.

It was Easter, Holy week, a time of new beginnings and fond memories with my Mom…Easter baskets and egg hunts. Startled by my phone ringing as I reminisced, I heard my brother say, "Our stepdad is in the hospital and dying of pancreatic cancer and is holding onto something." Standing shocked, speechless, my hands were trembling. I knew what that something was. I can't believe it was three years. *Trust Me,* I heard repeatedly inside my head. *Okay God, I get it. I know what I need to do.* My son insisted on going with me to the hospital, as though he needed to protect me from any more pain. As we walked into the room, I was overcome with a sense of peace and strength. Our eyes met; he looked ashamed as his eyes filled with tears. "Hi, Grandpa," Nik said as he pulled up a chair next to the bed. It was as though my son already forgave his grandpa without saying it.

"May I sit here?" I asked as I sat on the bed.

It was as though everyone knew why we were there. The nurse left the room after I sat down, and the rest of the family members stayed in the hallway, leaving the three of us uninterrupted. His clearly spoken words, "Can you believe I have the same thing as your mother?" made it hard to believe he was dying anytime soon. I could easily tell he was struggling with what to say, maybe because Nik was sitting there, or too ashamed of his previous words and actions.

Grabbing his hand, I said, "I forgive you. Please let go and let God take you." We held hands and together recited the "The

Prayer." We hugged, said our goodbyes, and lastly, I said, "I love you. I forgive you. It's time to let go." He passed away, on Easter Sunday.

After the loss of my mother and stepfather, I felt God's presence during the early morning hours when I had trouble sleeping. Powerful healing messages filled my heart—God was talking, and I was listening. I saw messages as images of simple words that spoke volumes; "Let Go Let God," "I AM," and "Broken Not Shattered."

God created these images, thus creating Inspirational Visions, LLC (www.inspirationalvisionsllc.com). Inspirational Visions is my small business offering big and powerful messages—simple messages applied on various products. The messages speak differently to each person, messages reminding us, we are not broken or alone when we let go and let God. It also provides a blog filled with hope and encouraging stories.

By the guidance of the Holy Spirit, my brokenness turned to a breakthrough, and my life messes turned into powerful messages, ones that reflect something different to each individual—whatever may be going on in his or her life at the time:

"Let Go Let God." Let go of worry and put everything in God's hands.

"I AM" God is telling me He is the vine, we are His branches; He is the center of our lives and wants positive affirmations to flow through our veins, and to know we are Beautiful, Holy, Loved, Confident, Caring…

"Broken Not Shattered" When we let go, God shows us how the light shines through our brokenness, and we are no longer the shattered negative pieces of our lives.

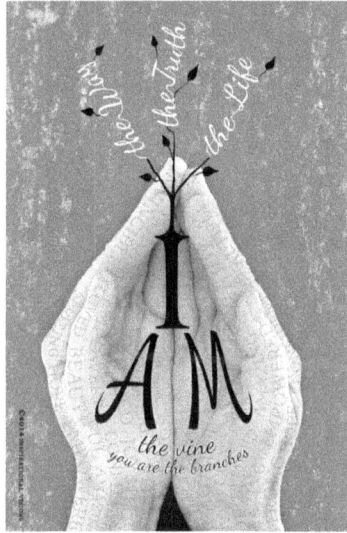

Scrapbook

Mom & me

Mom and me in Mexico.
Our last vacation together

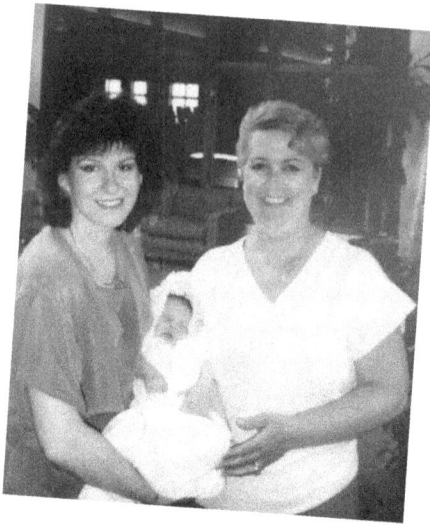

A Blessing

Three generations

Mom & Michelle

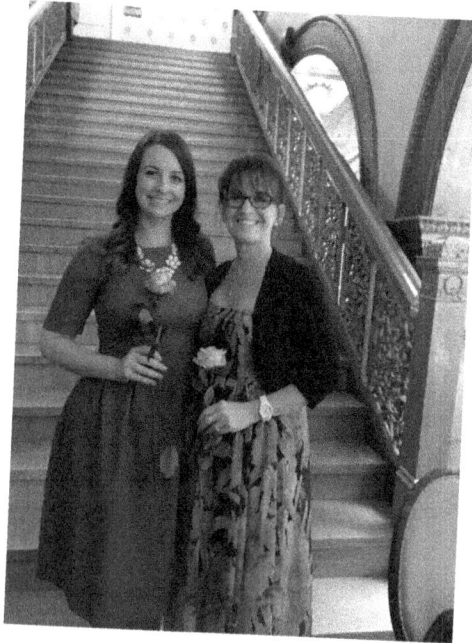

With Michelle on Mother's Day

My Mother - My Best Friend

Knowledge and wisdom are gifts you've shared
you've been there for me and always cared
my broken heart you took time to mend
still learning from you and will to the end
you've taught me to love and be a good mother
no one will compare - there'll be no other
you're one of a kind full of laughter and tears
I'll always remember each day and each year
though there were miles that kept us apart
it never changed the love in your heart
God brought me back it was part of His plans
and by your side I will always stand
I love you today like never before
I'll love you tomorrow and forevermore.

Love,
Mary

Oct. 2012

Poem I wrote for Mom When She Passed

CHAPTER SIX

PIETY

A genuine religious spirit turning to the Father as
His child and having a love for others

The Gift
of Life

I praise you because I am fearfully and wonderfully made; your works are wonderful, I know that full well.

Psalm 139:14 NIV

MANY GIFTS—DIFFERENT PACKAGES

What does the gift of life mean to you? Is it seeing a baby born?
Becoming a Believer? A new day? Words from a reading or prayer?
It's a meaning or definition that can change at any given time.

Our days are never promised. God already has our journey and our road map planned out. Although the journey will include serving Him, He gives us choices. Have you ever had something happen and thought, *This is it! Today is the last day on earth. Now what? Do you reflect back how you could have done things differently? Does the cliché, "If I only knew then what I know now" ever cross your mind?*

Upon reflection: *When I first moved to Colorado, I flew back to Arizona to surprise and celebrate a friend's spa grand opening. Upon my return, I noticed what I thought was an ingrown hair on the right side of my leg. It was a slightly raised red circle, smaller than a pencil eraser. It itched at first and then became painful and turned into a constant throbbing pain. By the next week I woke up to a larger, more swollen circle, even more painful. My diagnosis at Urgent Care was cellulitis, and I received a penicillin shot. The doctor marked the infected red circle with a black marker and said if the infection went outside the markings, get to your regular physician ASAP. Ok, now I was a little scared!*

The initial scare became even scarier. The red circle got much larger and more painful. I was put on antibiotics and the waiting began. After seven days, no positive change took place, so another antibiotic was prescribed. It was another seven days, and still nothing. I tried a total of four different antibiotics which actually gave this infection even more time to grow internally. I went to my regular physician, a dermatologist, and then an infectious disease doctor when the infection abscessed. By this time the infection was so deep that the shot given to numb the area prior to draining the abscess did not work, and the level of pain was indescribable. I felt every scrape and movement as though I was going through an out-of-body experience and living during the old western days and wishing I had a shot of whiskey and a bullet between my teeth to help tolerate the pain. I remember calling my mom afterwards and asking if she could hear me all the way in Wisconsin. I was crying so hard, she no longer could understand me.

The doctors were convinced that after another 10 to 14 days I could look back at this experience as it being a bad nightmare, and I would be healed.

The pain was getting worse and at a time when others were counting their blessings and being thankful, I was questioning why I was given such pain and heading to the hospital Thanksgiving morning when I woke up to blister-like sores all over my leg. What the heck was going on with me Lord? I know, I'm supposed to put all this in God's hands, but I'm scared, and confused why this isn't going away and wondering why doctors do not know what is wrong with me?

Even the doctors at the hospital were confused. They took a biopsy of the fluid from the blisters and sent me home.

That weekend my friend Patti-Jo (the one I thought would never be my friend in eighth grade, when I moved back with my mom; well...we're still best friends!) called me to see how I was doing. Patti-Jo loved to do research to find out the "Why's?" While on our computers and phone, Patti-Jo asked about my symptoms; just like many of us, we want immediate answers to "why" we feel the way we do. Upon her research, Patti-Jo found an article about MRSA. According to mayoclinic.org, Methicillin-resistant Staphylococcus aureus (MRSA) is a bacterium that causes infections in different parts of the body. Generally, MRSA starts as swollen, painful red bumps that might resemble pimples or spider bites. These can quickly turn into deep, painful abscesses that require surgical draining. Sometimes the bacteria remain confined to the skin. But they can also burrow deep into the body, causing potentially life-threatening infections in bones, joints, surgical wounds, the bloodstream, heart valves, and lungs.

"Mary, this article describes everything you have," Patti-Jo stated.

"Well, we will just have to wait and see if that's what the doctors find out," I replied.

The telephone rang on Sunday and it was a call from the hospital, which surprised me on a Sunday.

"Is this Mary?" The nurse asked.

"Yes," I responded.

"You have MRSA and need to be put on a new antibiotic because your body resisted all the other ones," she told me.

I started my new antibiotics right away. Once again, it was out of my control, and I had to let go and put this in God's hands.

The next day, I called my friend Patti-Jo and attempted to tell her what they said, but all that came out was, "Patti-Jo, I don't feel well."

"What is wrong? You're slurring your words! I'm coming over! I'll be there in 20 minutes. If you can, call the internal medicine doctor's office and tell them you are coming in," said Patti-Jo.

As soon as she walked into my house, she took one look at me and said, "Mary, I have never seen you like this! You look weak and lethargic." We are going to the doctor now! Patti-Jo was adamant about racing me to the internal medicine doctor's office, one I had seen weeks prior. I was getting weaker and weaker during the drive. While sitting in the doctor's office, slumped over, Patti-Jo repeated, "Mary, I have known you since eighth grade, and I have never seen nor heard you talk like this! You're not making sense." The doctor walked in and asked who Patti-Jo was and I blurted out (in slurred speech), "She's my medical voice!"

Patti-Jo did all the talking and repeated our history to him. She begged him to admit me into the hospital. He suggested that we give the antibiotics more time to do what they are meant to do. That answer was unacceptable to Patti-Jo. She said, "I think she has MRSA and needs to be admitted!" Apparently at that time, he hadn't yet received the information from the other hospital.

"What makes you think that?" He asked.

"EITHER YOU ADMIT HER OR I AM TAKING HER TO EMERGENCY! THIS IS NOT MARY, AND SHE IS NOT MAKING SENSE!" Patti-Jo bellowed at the doctor.

He called over to admitting, and Patti-Jo got a wheelchair and wheeled me over.

I was admitted to the hospital, and, to the doctor's surprise, my blood pressure dropped and it took 24 attempts to get an IV in me, even the emergency room IV experts had to be called because I was so dehydrated.

Being I was so weak and in so much pain, I truly thought I was dying. Many doctors and surgeons came in to discuss options. The first step was to have an MRI to see how deep the MRSA was. Results: the severity of the infection was a hairline above my bone.

"We can cut out the infection," one doctor said.

That sounded easy, just cut out the infection, and I'll be back to normal.

"What does that mean exactly?" I asked.

"We would amputate from the knee down or cut the portion of your leg that is infected which is just below your right knee all the way to your ankle and to the bone."

"WHAT!!!!! Like literally carve my leg out, and then what? Walk around with half of my leg missing?"

"Yes! But you would be alive, and still have both legs." The doctor replied.

I may have been weak, but God was not done with me. He gave me enough strength to say, "What is another option? I don't like that one!"

"You can be hooked up to the strongest IV antibiotic there is, called Vancomycin, while you're here this week and then we will order another MRI, and see if there is any progress. Then, we will put a PICC line in, and you will have to administer the IV antibiotic twice a day, every day, for a month or longer depending on how long it takes to kill the infection."

It seemed like the longest week of my life. But if I could keep my leg, and this IV antibiotic worked, then I would be very happy.

By this time, anyone who came into the room had to wear a yellow gown, mask, and gloves. Patti-Jo was a blessing. She was there as much as she could be.

During that week, a twenty-one-year-old athlete died of MRSA. I wondered if I was next. I put my life in God's hands.

At the end of my ten days in the hospital, the new MRI showed progress so I was able to keep my entire leg and administer the Vancomycin myself.

God had a plan. I needed to be patient, and trust Him.

Patti-Jo was my gift! God put her in my life and gave me a chance to live longer and serve His purpose.

Within two years, after another stressful time in my life, I started to get lumps in my groin area and Patti-Jo encouraged me to see my doctor right away. The "how" it came back is unknown, but sure enough, I ended up with my second round of MRSA and ended up back in the hospital. This time, they caught it early enough and the Vancomycin took care of it!

For I know the plans I have for you," declares the LORD, "plans to prosper you and not to harm you, plans to give you hope and a future. Jeremiah 29:11 (NIV)

For it is by grace you have been saved, through faith—and this is not from yourselves, it is the gift of God. Ephesians 2:8 (NIV)

God had plans for me and through His grace, not only gave me the gift of life, but the gift of having children, family, friends, and a compassionate, and caring heart.

My compassion and caring heart led me to writing. During the tough time of watching my mom's life come to an end, I was energized through my short nights by writing poems while the children slept. Every morning, my mom and I would talk and her first question she asked was, "Well, Honey, how many poems did you write?" She waited eagerly to hear me read them to her. I could hear in her voice she was feeling the same peace I had come to know.

My mom was my biggest fan, supporter, and cheerleader! Even through her pain, suffering, and knowing her days were fewer than we wanted, she kept a positive attitude, and encouraged me to keep writing. She told me it was my gift, and she wanted to hear them all. We laughed, cried, and soaked up every moment we could. This was a precious time in my life that no one could ever take away from me.

The poem, *My Mother – My Best Friend*, was the first one I wrote for her as it describes her the best and the nature of our relationship:

My Mother – My Best Friend

Knowledge and wisdom are gifts you've shared

you've been there for me and always cared.

My broken heart you took time to mend,

still learning from you and will to the end.

You've taught me to love and be a good mother

no one will compare – there'll be no other.

You're one of a kind, full of laughter and tears.

I'll always remember each day and each year.

Though there were miles that kept us apart

it never changed the love in your heart.

God brought me back it was part of His plan

and by your side I will always stand.

I love you today like never before.

I'll love you tomorrow and forevermore.

My mother was my gift. I was blessed to have her by my side no matter where or how far I lived from her; she taught me so many life lessons and comforted my broken heart. Her selfless, non-judgmental attitude and compassion for others was the legacy she left for me to carry on for her.

Although losing someone you love isn't easy, instead of looking at it as the end or death, look at the gift of life left behind in other ways. It is the light of her memory forever in my heart. It is carrying on with her teachings and wisdom. It is the light of her traits shining through another.

As Jesus died for us and suffered the pain of our sins, He gave us His light (the gift of life) and parable teachings (moral and spiritual lessons) to be in our thoughts, words, actions, and in our hearts to share with others. We are to be His disciples, loving one another as He loves us. We are to share our gifts of life with one another.

Four years after my mother passed away, I received the gift of a proposal in marriage to the wonderful man God gifted me with 30,000 feet in the air.

Although planning our wedding celebration was exciting, there was still deep sadness in my heart…not having my mom present as well as finding out my son would be deployed right before the wedding, and he'd be unable to attend. It left an emptiness in my heart. It wasn't perfect, but I was still happy and excited to finally marry my best friend, the man who loved me unconditionally, my gentle giant, and the one who God gave me. Everything continued as planned.

Wait!

Did I say, planned?

Life never goes as planned. Something or someone changes everything, good, bad, or different. That beautiful, sunny, planning afternoon in February, only four months before the wedding, turned dark and gloomy like an unexpected thunderstorm rolling in faster than ever.

We all sat in the doctor's office, my brothers, sister-in-law, father, and I all waited for the news.

"He has less than two years to live," the doctor said soberly.

WHAT?

How can this be? We are planning my wedding, everyone is finally getting along, which wasn't always the case. Now a big decision had to be made. Two brothers and myself needed to be tested. Who would be a match? What does all this mean? The youngest of my brothers was diagnosed with Myelofibrosis and needed a bone marrow transplant. He was given less than two years survival rate.

Each of us went into the lab to get our blood drawn. I remember my heart racing, and somehow I felt, deep down, I would be the match. The thought of being able to save my brother's life would be a true miracle. The waiting game began.

Later that week, while at work, my cell phone rang; I grabbed it quickly and ran into the hallway for privacy.

"Hello, this is the nurse from Froedtert's Oncology Department. Is this Mary?" the voice said.

"Yes." I said confidently.

"Mary, you are a match! You were the ONLY match!" the nurse told me.

I stood in the hallway shocked, as tears ran down my cheeks.

"I can actually save my brother?" I surprisingly asked.

The nurse said, "This is your decision to make and no one, absolutely no one, knows you are a match right now. Let me share the details with you and what you will go through."

She proceeded to share: I would get a shot in my stomach for a few days producing bone marrow, and then they would draw the bone marrow out through my veins. All I could think about was, *I'm going to save my brother's life*!

"Ok!" I exclaimed.

This sounds easy enough. I take a couple of shots, get the bone marrow taken out, and my brother gets to live. Perfect! I'll do it.

She repeated, "This is still your decision to make, and no one knows you are a match."

"OK! OK! I get it." Obviously, she knew more about the risks for both of us. It would have been better if we were the same sex, but like life, it's never perfect. It was a risk we needed to take. I never worried. I knew we were in God's hands!

I confirmed my "YES" and moved forward as the donor. The wedding plans continued as the doctor confirmed there wasn't any urgency in doing this prior to the wedding.

He said, "Get married, go on your honeymoon, and enjoy yourself; we will set everything up for late summer."

Towards the end of July, I received a call from the Cancer Center. Preparation, testing, and scheduling began. I had already researched and asked a lot of questions about the process. I was told many donors get their injections and go back to work. Everything was an outpatient procedure. *No problem. I can handle that! I'm going to save my brother's life; it'll all be worth it.*

I thought I was receiving one injection for five days, not one "set" of injections for five days. After the second set of subcutaneous injections in my abdomen, I began feeling weak. By the third set, I felt as though I was a slumped-over, frail, 100-year-old lady. I couldn't work or concentrate. Thank God for my husband. He was not only my support but my strength and interpreter. He never left my side. I had two more sets of injections before the apheresis process, which is similar to donating plasma. A needle was placed in each of my arms. Blood was removed from my vein in one arm and passed through tubing into a blood cell separator machine. The machine collected the blood-forming cells, platelets, and some white blood cells. Plasma and red blood cells were returned to my body through my other arm. The nurse told me this process could take up to eight hours, and I would be unable to move, not even to go to the bathroom, until the process was complete. At that point, I was so weak, I just wanted this out of my body, to help my brother, and for everyone to feel better. Little did I know within minutes of being hooked up, my tiny veins could not handle the pressure of the draw as the needle came out and blew my vein.

What now? How would the medical team get these cells to come out of me if they can't come out of my veins?

The only other option was to place a central venous line into one of my larger veins, such as the jugular or subclavian vein.

According to the National Marrow Donor Program ("NMDP") only 19 percent of women and 3 percent of men have ever gone through this process. Nonetheless, it was the only process that would work for me.

"We'll be right back," said the nurse as she took me to another cold, sterile hospital room.

Craig waited in the hospital room while I was wheeled down the hall. *I'm scared. What does all this mean? Are they going to put me under? How do they go into the jugular or subclavian vein? So many questions with no complete answers.*

The door opened; the room was cold and looked like a stainless steel surgery room. Everything happened so fast. My clouded mind only remembers three of us in the room. One nurse held my hand as I squeezed as tight as possible, then I was instructed by the other nurse and doctor, "This will hurt like hell!" (*which it did*), "Squeeze as hard as you need to!" (*and I did!*)

In a matter of seconds, so it seemed, all the questions were answered and back to the blood cell separator machine. The process of how this machine separated my cells and then put them back into my body amazed me. The pain was gone, and my blessings counted. I could now save my brother's life. I was so grateful to be chosen. The doctors decided to leave the central venous line in until the next day, just in case they needed more cells. The nurse

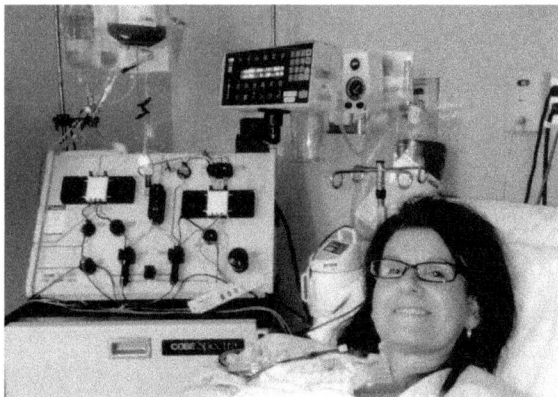

gave Craig discharge instructions, as my mind was still foggy. She said they would call Craig later and let him know if they received enough cells.

Right before bedtime, he received the call. They got enough! What a celebration and a gift to give! Because we lived so far from the hospital, they said I wouldn't need to go back that night to get the line removed. They set up a time the next day and gave Craig instructions on how to care for me that night. I knew I would sleep like a baby after all this emotional stress. In the middle of the night I had to get up to use the bathroom but could feel my hair was wet.

I woke Craig up and he said, "Don't move!" He jumped out of bed, turned on the light and calmly said, "Honey, don't move; I'll be right back." Still feeling pretty weak, I knew I wasn't going to be jumping up or going anywhere. I felt like a wet noodle. Thank God for my husband Craig and his ability to remain calm, cool, and collected while cleaning up and bandaging my neck from the blood loss coming from the irritated line. Only God knew what could have happened that night had Craig not been there. I was in God's hands.

On September 25, 2012, we watched my cells go through an IV as they entered my brother's body. Tears flowed and prayers were said. Only God knew if this would work and save his life. Today, he is alive, well, and blessed to hold his beautiful granddaughter… the true meaning of the Gift of Life!

God guides us through our sufferings and our pains become our blessings. Everything happens for a reason.

Everything that happens in this world happens at the time God chooses. He sets the time for birth and the time for death, the time for planting and the time for pulling up. Ecclesiastes 3:1-2(GNT)

"...let them learn first to show piety toward their own family..."
1 Timothy 5:4 (ASV)

CHAPTER SEVEN

KNOWLEDGE

Seeing things from God's perspective

Perspective

or

Perception

God makes everything happen at the right time. Yet none of us can ever fully understand all He has done, and He puts questions in our minds about the past and the future.

- Ecclesiastes 3:11 CEV

DON'T JUDGE THE STORY BY THE
CHAPTER YOU WALKED INTO

This reminds me of the time I walked into the living room and found a dining room chair pulled up next to the fish tank. Sitting on the edge of the couch with a completely blank and innocent look was my two-year old son. He looked like, *Who me? I didn't do anything…really I didn't!*

When I asked where all the fish were, his eyes welled up, bottom lip quivered, and as his head looked down, he said, "I..I..I just wanted them to be my friends!"

"Honey, its ok, I know! Just tell mommy where the fish are," I said in a calm but frantic voice.

Slowly he bent forward and began to lift the edge of the table runner up on the coffee table. There they all lay, one perfectly in line with the other. *There is no way these fish will still be alive,* I thought. Without startling my son, I quickly grabbed the fish net and said, "Oh, Honey, they need water to live. They can be your friends, but they need to be your friends while living in the fish tank." I scooped them up quickly, put them back into the fish tank and prayed they would be alive. Those fish were in God's hands, and each and every one of them survived. In his little mind, his perception was that he could play with these fish until his sister came home from school.

Our timing and/or perception can change everything. Are we in the right place at the right time or listening to what is specifically meant for our ears to hear? It's all part of our journey!

Have you ever questioned why someone came into your life at *that* moment for *that* reason? Why *now*? What does *this* mean?

CHANGE IS IN THE AIR

The positive change I needed wasn't happening while working at the law firm. My perspective of my purpose there changed. I knew if the good Lord brought me to it, He would help me through it. At this point, my friendships were the only positive connection to the job. Whether I talk to a friend once a day, week, month or year(s); a friend is a friend forever, to me. This time I needed to make a change and God opened another door. Taking another job only changed the skills I was using, it didn't change my friends. Although I enjoyed teaching Pre-K, I thought getting back into the school system would be a better fit for me. I could still teach, just in different ways. While I've heard some say you start at the bottom and work your way up. I started at the top, in the District Office. Who defines bottom or top? Is one better than the other? I personally say, "It's all in your perspective."

Her smile lit up the room and her laugh was contagious. She was beautiful inside and out. She was the co-op student, office helper…everyone seemed to have some common thread that ran through the office, a commonality, if you will…everyone but me. I was the newbie. No common connection to the school, office, or area. Just me and them, although I felt a special connection with this curly haired, bubbly young girl in the office. I wondered. Why the connection? Who am I? She knows everyone, they all have history, and I have nothing in common with her.

A group of us headed into a conference room to begin working on a large mailing. She asked if she could put some music on while we worked. We all agreed. The minute I heard the first song, my eyes lit up like a Christmas tree, and before I knew it, I shouted, "Hey, I love this music!"

Our common thread…loving the same Christian music. From that moment on, our conversations were endless. She shared her faith, and I shared mine. God put us together for a reason. No longer feeling disconnected maybe? Or, was God confirming I was put there for a reason? When I left my previous job at the law firm, my attorney friend Jascha told me, "God has a plan for you, your job is done here!" I always wondered why he made that comment to me. Did God tell him to tell me that? Did he know something I didn't?

The beautiful, curly haired helper left for college. I'm sure I'll never see her again, I thought. She has a busy life ahead of her now! We kept in touch and would try our best to see each other when she came back into town from college. Whenever we were together, our conversations were raw, real, and authentic. We prayed, laughed, and cried together.

I'll never forget the day she changed my life and my perspective on the constant questions that ran through my head. She asked me to go to lunch. After we ate she said, "I have been praying for an answer to a question for some time now, and I get the same answer each time!"

"Victoria, you're so serious, you're scaring me," I said.

She responded, "I have been praying for a mentor in my life, and God gave me the answer."

"Oh, Honey, I am so happy for you." I said excitedly.

"It's you, Mary! God told me to ask you!" she exclaimed.

In shock, I responded as the tears fell gently down my cheek, "But Victoria, you know so many Godly people around the world;

you've helped many people, and are involved in so many Christian organizations, why me? How is it that He chose me to be your mentor?"

"Will you, Mary?" she asked.

I softly replied, "I would be honored…I am honored to be your mentor!"

That day, Victoria changed my life! God changed our lives! I no longer question why God puts someone in my life; I simply put everything in His hands and wait for guidance.

See, I am doing a new thing! Now it springs up; do you not perceive it? I am making a way in the wilderness and streams in the wasteland. Isaiah 43:19

OUR MASKS

Are you hiding behind a mask? Do you hide behind humor, sarcasm, or just plain shut down?

It was a perfect day to join friends for lunch. The sun was shining bright and the air crisp and cool; a typical spring afternoon on the outside while I felt awesome and peaceful on the inside. Negativity was not on my menu but apparently it was part of one of my friends. The negatively charged-jokes, sarcasm and insults flew out of his mouth like a storm of locusts. I needed a large flyswatter to kill them as fast as I heard them. But I had an even better weapon…God! He is my shield, my protector, and my strength. He's faster, stronger, and can defend against any negativity, thought, or action, faster than I can. In God's hands, I put this challenge.

What was supposed to be an enjoyable lunch with friends, became an unexpected challenge and debate about life, religion, faith, judging, etc.

Trust Him! I repeatedly heard, TRUST HIM!

Once again, I trusted God and did not judge.

I took a deep breath, trusted God to give me the words and actions to stay strong and fight the battle.

First question I asked, "Do you believe in God?"

"No, I'm agnostic! I don't have knowledge that God exists," my friend said.

I smiled and asked, "Do you see the air you breathe? Do you see the wind blow without looking at an object?" I confirmed, "God is like that. He is there, all around us. He created us. He is in each one of us and comes out through our smiles, kind words, actions, etc."

The seed was planted.

Through my experiences, I see these masks as results of having internal deep-seated pain. People may use humor or sarcasm to hide their pain. I see this in others, sometimes better than they can see it in themselves. Some may say this is a curse; I say it's a blessing.

I continued to listen to the unending questions. It was at that moment, while listening, that I could have easily perceived my faith and beliefs under attack, but God made me realize this person may have never had this type of conversation with anyone before.

God opened the door of opportunity for me to share my gifts, to help someone who is sensitive, anxious, insecure...WAIT...that described me. I once possessed all of those feelings; however, when I put my sensitive, anxious, and insecure traits in God's hands, I felt more confident, free, and loved.

I shared, "Fighting past the fear of the unknown is hard and scary and it makes us anxious. However, if we never journey outside of our own skin, move in an unknown direction, nothing changes; we stay in the same spot day after day, year after year. I challenge you to make one change. Believe in yourself and say, "Yes, I can!" Doing something good and positive is better than nothing at all. A change, no matter how small, will give you hope to see your journey differently. God wants us to change, be closer to Him and trust Him when we let go and let God. Surrender your anxieties, and put your life in His hands. You may not completely believe in God, but questioning gives me hope that you will continue to feel alive and confident when you peel away, one layer at a time, the negative layers of what the world or your past has made you believe. Each layer you peel away gets rid of the negativity and allows you to get to the core of your being; and allows you to find the treasure and becoming the real, raw, and authentic YOU that God created. You're in His hands! Just believe!"

I could see the wheels spinning as the questions stopped and the mental process began.

I proceeded to share some of my own personal stories and struggles and how my faith has helped me. We learned that our perspective on things was different, which doesn't make one better than the other, or one right and the other wrong; it gives us the ability to look at things differently, with new options. I call it planting seeds of awareness. The walls started slowly coming down, and I had no idea how sharing my faith, stories, or options could have such an impact on one individual. The negativity, sarcasm, judgment, and hatred turned into positivity, giving him an understanding everyone has a story, and transforming him into a caring and compassionate person who said…

"Mary has an amazing way of providing other options without pressuring or forcing them. I am able to open up and be myself with her because she never judges me no matter what I have done or what I shared. It was crucial to see Mary lead by example and not just speak empty words, always treating others with respect and without judgment. Mary has a way of encouraging me to be a better person without pushing me, and she NEVER gave up on me. This was so vital because it wouldn't have worked for me. I would have put my walls up to prevent what I always felt was an attack and criticism of who I was. I have been told what to do and how to be my entire life, and I was tired of being pushed. I wanted to make my own decisions, but unfortunately this backfired as I took it to the extreme. For the past five years, I decided to be negative and judgmental and held onto so much hatred. I would constantly play devil's advocate and argue with people and purposely take a different viewpoint just to prove a point. I'm still not sure what point I was trying to prove. I was sick and tired of following others so, that was my reaction and response."

Mary would show me other paths and viewpoints I could choose to follow and believe. It was never about telling me what to see or believe, and she did it in such a way that didn't cause me to be defensive. It takes a special person to be able to do that and that's the reason why Mary is such a great mentor."

In a short time, I noticed little changes. No more sarcasm, a lot more inquiries, less negative comments, no more swearing and a hopeful attitude.

Listening through someone's pain by explaining options or by looking at things differently, gives them a new light (God's light, they just may not know it yet) by changing their thoughts and actions.

And we know that all things work together for good to them that love God, to them who are the called according to his purpose. Romans 8:28 King James Version (KJV)

All this is for your benefit, so that the grace that is reaching more and more people may cause thanksgiving to overflow to the glory of God. 2 Corinthians 4:15 (NIV)

GOD WORKS IN MYSTERIOUS WAYS

God uses us, even when we don't always realize it at the time. Witnessing the changes in my friend made me reflect how God used my mess to create those powerful messages…the constant simple reminders to "Let Go Let God" (God is in control); "I AM" (God created us to feel beautiful, holy, and loved); and "Broken Not Shattered" (God shines His light and breaks through our no-longer-shattered life). God created these images for people to take away what they need…for whatever they are going through.

My angel Victoria gave me a name of a graphic designer, Gillian Miller, to create what the Holy Spirit described to me in the middle of the night. This was no ordinary graphic designer.

Gillian was a gift, an angel, a godly woman, and a very gifted artist. Each time we met to discuss my dream and how she would create it, I felt even more blessed. We shared our faith and our friendship. Our conversations were endless, and our friendship continued to grow. We both prayed, and she said God led her to painting the "Broken Not Shattered" image. It depicts the shattered, negative words the world, at one time or another, makes us feel or believe, and when we let go and let God, His light shines through our brokenness for us to be the beautiful, holy, loved, real, raw, and authentic one God created us to be.

God leads us to serve others in many different ways. God chose Victoria and led me to Gillian, which I thought was only to help me design the images; however, He led us to share our faith with one another, to help others, and feed the homeless. Victoria and Gillian both volunteered at a shelter in Milwaukee called Despensa de la Paz and invited me to join them. What struck me the most was how God directed my steps to volunteer with these two angels; however, their schedules pulled them away after our first day together, and then it was as though we alternated our days. Our purpose wasn't for us to be there together, it was to serve others. I have served at soup kitchens before, so in my mind, my perspective, I was going to serve at a "soup kitchen" in Milwaukee. It was to my pleasant surprise that this was a much bigger operation than I ever imagined. It had so many components to it which included: a "checker" (checking people in), a "bagger" (putting grocery bags together), a "runner" (walking the guests to get the appropriate number of grocery bags for the number of people in their family), serving coffee, fellowship, or going with the "StreetLife" team. This experience changed me and my heart, giving me a deeper love and appreciation for how God works in our lives.

There were many serving options at Despensa de la Paz. This particular Saturday I was asked to be part of the "StreetLife" team. I had no idea what that meant but because I was serving others, I went willingly. I got into a truck, and we drove to downtown Milwaukee. We set up tables in the Wells Fargo Bank parking lot, with permission of course. We set out sandwiches on the tables; obviously by the number of sandwiches made, this was not their first time. It reminded me of the fish and bread Bible story. No matter how many people arrived, there was plenty of food to go around. There was also hot coffee, personal hygiene products, and within the blink of an eye, the parking lot was full of homeless people needing a meal, hygiene products, and fellowship. We were their family. While the other volunteers were graciously providing for these homeless people, I was asked by one of the leaders if I was comfortable taking a long walk and feeding those who couldn't make it there? He knew their stories, and it wasn't for me to judge…just serve.

"Of course, I will go!" I excitedly said.

We walked for blocks and took several bagged lunches and left them in these hidden places in the city. My heart was warm and yet sad for how these people lived. It put things in perspective. I asked a lot of questions as we walked back. I was mystified as to how these people find freedom from this homelessness. The leader explained that several of the ones he talked to have tried and because of their past history, having no support or ways to make money, no one will hire them, and the vicious cycle continues.

There has to be a way!

FLASHBACK

This reminded me of the time our family drove to San Diego from Arizona. Nik was in Pre-K and Michelle in second grade. We came upon a homeless woman sitting on the concrete alongside a bridge overlooking the Bay. She wasn't begging for food but it was clear she didn't have anything to eat. Both Nik and Michelle eagerly said, "We should give her something to eat." It sounded like a great idea until I said, "We only have a box of Nik's favorite "CatDog" crackers in the backpack." Although Nik did not want to give up his favorite crackers, his hesitancy changed in an instance as he looked at what he had verses what she had. He took his box and together they walked over and gave her the box of crackers. She slowly opened the box. The priceless look on her face gave way to one of gratitude and confusion. She took out two crackers, put one in each hand and stared at the crackers, looking as though she was trying to figure out what she was beginning to eat. I'm confident to say, it was the first time she ever laid eyes on a "CatDog" cracker.

END OF FLASHBACK

We jumped back in the truck and while heading back to the center, we approached a traffic light. A homeless man was holding a sign that said "Hungry" and the leader rolled down his window, and yelled out, "Hey Bob, how are you doing?" He then motioned the homeless guy to meet us around the corner. We pulled over and the leader opened up backpacks of nonperishable food items including: canned fruit, snacks, etc. Bob's eyes were so big and lit up…I didn't know who was going to cry more…him or me! He was so grateful, thanked us many times over, and only took what he was given.

Our job was done, or so I thought. We had one more stop. We pulled over to the side of the road not far from one of the bridges.

"Wait here." the driver told me.

He ran jeans and food down under the bridge, and on his way back this large African-American man approached us and said, "Hey! How are you?" They hugged, and I was introduced. We shook hands and the three of us talked like we knew each other for years. He too, was very grateful for whatever was given to him, and the appreciation was written all over his smile. As we headed back I was so grateful myself for this opportunity to make a difference and help these homeless people feel beautiful, holy, and loved.

God continued to use Victoria to plant seeds of helping the broken. She also shared her experiences of helping the homeless in our own community through Family Promise.

Family Promise is a nonprofit organization helping homeless families towards a sustainable future. There are thirteen churches that rotate weekly, providing homeless families a warm place to sleep, hot meals to eat, and great fellowship from Sunday to Sunday.

A year and a half after Victoria shared her Family Promise experience, the church I belonged to had the opportunity to become a host church. In a room full of approximately 45 people, they asked for someone to step forward to be a coordinator. I could see the look on my husband's face, *No Mary, don't you do this, this is a huge commitment.* But I felt pulled by the Holy Spirit to stand up for what I believed in and said, "Yes, I will be a coordinator for St. Theresa's Parish."

Coordinating our host weeks could not be possible without the help of all the amazing volunteers God blessed us with. I call the volunteers "angels," because they are angels sharing their gifts to provide guest room setup, prepare meals, be a dinner host, an overnight host, or takedown volunteer. They work quarterly to make our Family Promise Host weeks huge successes. Many hands make light work. As we serve God and help others, we learn to put life in perspective. We long for so much, and they have so little; we long to be around missing family and/or friends and they are so grateful to have someone to talk to who cares. These are people who, just like anyone of us, have had an unfortunate circumstance in their lives, forcing them to reach out for help. We are their resource, friend, mentor, warm place, and seed planters. We respect where they are spiritually, without forcing our beliefs on them. Inspirational Visions LLC gifts a "Let Go Let God" magnet which is placed in their room basket. I remind them that everything in the basket is theirs to keep, except for the towels. A magnet is never left behind. We witness their appreciation through their warm smiles, hugs, and grateful words of thanksgiving. We bond for one week and change each other's lives. Sunday becomes a bittersweet day. We miss them as they drive away and continue on their journey waiting to move into their new home and/or hear about a new job, and learn to let go and let God.

No matter what we go through in life, God is there, He never leaves us, and He loves us unconditionally. He is forgiving and wants us to turn to Him in time of need.

We all need God, especially when we are shattered by our brokenness. I was called to facilitate a Christian-based program called "Divorce and Beyond." This program helps divorced women know there is life after divorce. I have met incredible women who were so broken, and so convinced of what they told me: "There is absolutely no way I will get over this and be where you are, especially with your ex." Each woman I met, smiled again, recovered in leaps and bounds through her once shattered life, and felt, once again, beautiful, holy, and loved. These women are powerful and have realized there IS life after divorce.

I have always told my children they are beautiful, holy, and loved, and when they are struggling with something, to put it in God's hands. He is the one who will give us the strength and peace we need.

When my son was deployed, he was going through a tough time in his relationship. He took a walk to find that sacred place to be alone with God, a place no one would see his vulnerable self. He came across a park and in the distance saw a bench next to a large tree. He slowly looked around, and said to himself, *Good, no one in sight.* He sat down, face in his hands, and poured his heart and soul out to the Lord, when all of a sudden, he felt a gentle touch on his shoulder. Startled at first, he pulled himself together, looked up, and this angel said, "It'll be ok; do you want to talk about it?"

Was this his "Ellen?" An angel he never knew or would never see again, touched his heart and gave him the strength he needed at that time. Before he knew it, she was gone, and he never even knew her name.

He immediately called to tell me what had just happened to him.

"Mom, I had an "Ellen" angel experience, just like you!" Nik added.

Was this my "Ellen" helping him? I wondered.

Maybe my "Ellen" lived on the other side of the world. I opened the Bible I received from Ellen, contacted the Bible Institute and gave them her name and the date she would have attended, hoping to one day meet and thank her for being my inspired angel.

"Unfortunately, I've exhausted my ability to search with the information you provided. I can find no record of an Ellen Bennett; maybe she didn't finish the program and that is why I cannot find any information," said the representative from the Bible Institute.

God put Ellen in my life when He knew I needed His strength and faith to move forward. Look to see which angel God puts in your life today. It may be that well needed simple smile, heartfelt hug, or an act of kindness.

I wouldn't change my journey for anything in this world. These seven gifts from the Holy Spirit, (fortitude, understanding, hope, wisdom, counsel, justice, and knowledge) healed me from the wounds of a broken heart, abuse, losses, and struggles, and have given me the opportunity to meet incredible people, learn valuable lessons, and most importantly grow in my faith, and be blessed tenfold.

God is far from done with me. I know His plans are bigger than I will ever imagine. I look forward to this journey as my journey so far has given me the strength I never knew I had. Strength to share my story, giving God all the glory, and sharing my God-given gifts to not only bless my children, family and friends, but anyone God puts along my path, and to share this is a journey not our destination.

Our perception of our journey can be misconstrued if we try to control or have expectations. I am on a deeper level of my spiritual journey. As Thomas Keating has put it so nicely, "The transitional stage is always painful because we know only where we are now, and we are not always ready, especially in the beginning of our new journey, to move into the unknown. What we know is better than what we don't know. We resist the moment of creative change." I look forward to deepening my faith by consenting to God changing me. That means focusing on Him, not what the world expects of me, not to judge any chapter I walk into, not allowing the expectations, demands, or obstacles to get in the way of hearing the word of God. I want to release any attachment I have to my own ideas or plans and discipline myself to a deeper level that will give me peace and spiritual consolation and enable me to entrust God with my entire life story. We know that God already knows our plan, however, we need to trust in God to acknowledge the dark side of our personality, our motivation, and selfishness. Without this deep trust in God, we maintain our defense mechanisms.

I challenge you to deepen your trust in God and deepen your spiritual journey. Look at life, people, situations, etc., through God's eyes, and put everything in God's hands. God never promised us life would be painless, but He did promise us that with Him all things are possible. He led me through a life-changing journey, and I am still growing. Whenever a negative thought enters my mind, I turn it around to the positive and look for what God is revealing to me.

Seeing things from God's perspective gives you the knowledge that you are no longer shattered by your brokenness. You are Beautiful, Holy, and Loved. He is the Way, the Truth, and the Life;

He is the center of our lives, the vine and we are the branches. Let Go and Let God transform your life wherever you need it. He did mine!

He will be the sure foundation for your times, a rich store of salvation and wisdom and knowledge; the fear of the LORD is the key to this treasure. Isaiah 33:6 (NIV)

.

EPILOGUE

For he will command his angels concerning you to guard you in all your ways.

Psalm 91:11

IMPACTING LIVES

Do you ever wonder if what you said or did had any impact on someone?

Believe…people listening to your stories can have a bigger impact than you ever imagined, and come to fruition in God's timing. I never thought sharing the story I wrote for my religious education class, "No One was Homeless this Thanksgiving," with my mother-in-law would manifest my dreams and be a memorable birthday for me. I told her one day I would love to make that happen and how I would love everyone at our table to have a different patterned plate representing our differences. To my surprise, she gave me a set of hand-picked, different-patterned plates with cloth napkins for my birthday. The tears of joy and appreciation shocked everyone in the room. I finally felt heard. In 2019, our Family Promise Host Week is during Thanksgiving. It will be a blessing to give each guest his or her own patterned plate and cloth napkin, representing our differences and that we are one family under God, and no one is homeless this Thanksgiving. This is another example of one lesson impacting the lives of others.

This is just one of many examples of just when I think nobody is listening or I question if my sacrifices pay off, I am graciously reminded by a kind word or action I did or have done and how it makes a difference. I not only asked my children to write down things they have learned from me growing up and how that impacted their lives, but others who have had an incredible impact on my life, and how I impacted theirs. The answers I received were the best gifts. God has shown me there are no coincidences, and people come in and out of our lives for a reason. He has led me down this path, made me stronger through each trial, rejoiced in every triumph, healed my heart to love unconditionally, and that forgiveness isn't about the other person, it is a confirmation of my trust in God and being able to move forward. I've never given up hope, and I never will. I knew God would continue to give me the strength I needed; I needed to believe. He will give you too the strength to get through whatever is heavy on your heart. Hope is in the heart of the believer.

I am grateful for the opportunity to touch your lives. You never know what you say or do or how it will make a difference in someone's life. I never knew I had such an impact on these lives the way I have. I praise God for the gifts He has given me and give Him all the glory for using me to make a difference!

The "WHY" to the following quotes.

Like I have said throughout this book, everything happens for a reason and the people who cross your path in life are no different than the people who are meant to cross my path. I learned so much more about myself as I read each quote from just some of the people who have come into my life, not even realizing the difference or impact I made personally. This is an example of how God works in our lives. Each experience and/or person can have a lasting impression, leave a message, lesson or pass on the knowledge to see things from God's perspective.

What you do and/or say makes a difference.

TESTIMONIALS

"Life brings you good and bad but I have learned through my mom to stay strong through faith, trust your instincts and everything happens for a reason. God will always be with you."

Michelle H.

"I have learned from Mary surround yourself with people that love you and push you to be the best person possible."

Austin M.

"When I go through tough times, I think to myself, if my mom can be strong, forgiving, and have a positive attitude through everything she has been through, I can get through this!"

Nik Y.

"I've learned quite a bit from Mary, but one of the most important things has to do with love and family. She has taught me a lot about the importance of loving family, even during times when it's been difficult to like them. She has loved Austin and I as if we were her own children, even when we've gotten on her nerves. And Mary has shown such a capacity for giving unconditional love to many. She has been such an influence in my life and I'm sure the lives of many others."

Mitchell M.

"When I first sought a mentor, I prayed for a woman after God's heart whose model of prayerfulness, joy, and hope encouraged my faith. Additionally, I desired a woman who would challenge me and keep me accountable in my walk with the Lord. Watching Mary interact with others showed her selfless love rooted in Jesus' grace, and I wanted to spend as much time with her as possible! As Mary very openly shared with me parts of her life story, even some tough times, her trust in the Lord and her leaning on Him throughout all her stories testified to her faith and her hope in Christ Jesus.

When I asked Mary to be my mentor, I gained an invaluable advisor, prayer warrior, accountability partner, and second mom. Our mentorship relationship has evolved over time. In the beginning of our mentorship relationship, we saw each other daily! Now, separated by about 300 miles, we see each other as often as possible. Mary and I keep each other and each other's families in prayer often. Knowing I have a prayer warrior thinking of me multiple times a day encourages me to give to others in the same way! Mary is also a great reminder that the body of Christ is alive and well and that sisters and brothers in Christ extend far beyond blood ties. As she listens and advises and prays for me like a second mom, I appreciate learning from her life experiences and the way God works in her life! Mary's life stories of trials and temptations and God's faithfulness through it all serve as such encouragement and examples to me. In joyous times and times of hardship, I look to the Bible for similar stories proving God's faithfulness and forgiveness toward His beloved people over and over again. In addition, I seek out the wisdom of dear friends like Mary. Mary is amazing at listening and asking insightful questions that help me process my situations, encouraging me to be even more thankful to our heavenly Father and to lean on His truths even more. Mary is also amazingly empathetic and will cry and laugh and rejoice with me. Her genuine care for me reflects Jesus' love and forgiveness to me all the time!

I adore Mary as a friend, accountability partner, and second mom. I am so thankful for the family I've gained in Mary and all of the life experiences she has walked beside me and prayed with me in."

Victoria K.

"I have been taught so much from Mary that it is difficult to narrow it down, but the strongest thing that comes to mind is that I've learned to share my faith with others. Before I met Mary, my faith was personal. Over the years, Mary taught me how sharing my faith with others makes me accountable for my faith in action. I now openly share my faith with those around me and I've seen a difference not only in myself, but in my family and friends since I've started sharing my faith with them. They are now openly and joyfully sharing their faith too. Sharing faith with others has a ripple effect that can change the world, one person at a time. I know my world changed the day I met my dear friend Mary Markham."

Cathy C.

"Sometimes our best support and needs are fulfilled by friends and family who come through marriage, rather than being blood relatives. Choose those who make you happy and love you for who you are."

Debbie M.

"I met Mary in middle school and we couldn't have been more different. We grew up under very different circumstances and despite these differences, we grew to view each other as "family." Our signature 1979 song was "We Are Family" by Sister Sledge. Dancing around the room and singing our anthem song bonded us for years to come. As we blurted out the words to the song 'here is our golden rule, have faith in the things you do, you won't go wrong, this is our family jewel,' we could have never imagined how those words would ring true. Faith in God, faith in yourself to overcome the challenges of life, the permission to rejoice in all things good, and the support of 'family,' these are the life lessons we've lived through our relationship."

Patti-Jo V.

"It will be difficult to focus in on one thing that I've learned during our many years of friendship, but if I had to pick the one thing that has impacted me the most, it would be Mary's capacity to love. Mary is the most giving and kind person I've ever had known. I see the love shining through her eyes to whomever she is focused on. That has made me want to open my heart to others as willingly as I have witnessed from Mary, my very dear friend."

Deby C.

"I am blessed God has placed such a faith-filled woman in my life! Always, walking with God on our earthly journey. Mary will inspire you by her listening ears and loving heart. Joyful, kind, and loving. Humbly working God's works."

Julie Z.

"I have learned from Mary the wonder of sharing her faith with others. Her thoughtful insights and passion for humanity have given me and others the courage to be brave and share God's word. She encourages all to trust that God will give you the grace to know what to say and what to do to provide hope to others in their daily lives. Mary is a very strong woman whose faith in God and all that is good resonates and penetrates those around her to help them see light and feel peace."

Deb R.

"I have learned a LOT from Mary. One of the major lessons I have learned over the years of knowing Mary is that the best kind of a life we can lead is a God-centered life. Mary taught me to BELIEVE that we are each on a path that has been laid out in front of us by God. When things seem tough, it is human nature to question Him and ask, 'why me, God?' But then I remember what Mary has always said: have faith that you are exactly where you are supposed to be on your path. She has been through a LOT and has hung on to her faith and beliefs that she was exactly where she was supposed to be. I have adopted that same belief and have also passed it along to my children. It has gotten all of us through some pretty rough times. Which I guess you can say brings me to something else I have learned from Mary: through faith and living a God-centered life, all things are possible. We are all living proof of that and my dear friend, Mary Markham, not only talks this talk, but she walks that walk."

Chris S.

"I feel like there have been pivotal people in my life that have left their footprints in my life path and Mary is definitely one of them. I loved watching her be brave and achieve her goals. I remember her feeling apprehensive about going to college and then while in college the joy she had in writing and excelling in college. I have always remembered that and felt some kindred to her when I endeavored something I needed to be brave about also. There is no age limit as to when we stop growing and I hope I always have her infectious positive manner to conquer my adventures in life."

Lorene E.

"A long time ago Mary replied to a thread of emails going around St. Theresa's regarding Family Promise. Mary said, (and it stuck with me): *'I accept my calling as a Christian and Disciple, doing God's works, and will continue to help others in any way I can.'* I printed it and it hangs on my bulletin board to remind me, that as disciples, we face challenges every day. Thank you, Mary, for being a wonderful friend and mentor to so many."

Judy H.

"I cherish the friends we have become and see through Mary's eyes and kind loving self she has for others. Family is a magical part of who she is, and always puts them first.

Mary's strength within makes people happy. She is always ready to listen and always ready to offer support and encouragement! I appreciate and love her and wish her so much happiness!"

Connie M.

"God's plan for you is far better than the one you may have for yourself."

Jascha W.

"Not only has Mary been an influential friend, but she has been an angel to me. During adversity or turmoil, she always guides me to shift my focus on strength, hope, and faith."

Natalie M.

After reflecting upon my journey, and knowing I did the best I could raising my children, I asked Michelle and Nik, not to share with each other, but send me a list of at least five things they learned from me that they apply in their adult life. To my surprise, and again, without each other knowing, they began their list with the exact message. This list is a gift from God. I put my life in His hands and He guided me to teach them these messages, which will be a gift to future generations. I encourage you to ask the child(ren) in your life to share the gifts they have learned from you. You too, might be surprised.

Michelle wrote: Things I learned from my mom:

> *Treat other people the way you want to be treated.*
>
> *Every day is a school day (this has taught me to be humble and that always wanting to learn is a good thing).*
>
> *Love unconditionally.*
>
> *Give more than you receive.*
>
> *When something negative is going on in your life, someone has it worse.*
>
> *Your family is who you make it, and family comes first.*
>
> *Finding the positive in everything.*
>
> *How to be kind and giving by helping others in need.*
>
> *How to explore and be adventurous.*
>
> *Confident in meeting new people/learning how to make new friends.*
>
> *Being emotional and knowing that is okay.*

Nik Wrote: Things I learned from my mom:

Treat others the way you want to be treated.

Always go with your gut feeling.

Believe in fate; everything happens for a reason.

Although it's hard sometimes, be the bigger person and take the "high road." You'll feel better about the situation in the end.

Stand up for what you believe in.

Not to let what is classified as "normal" control you. Be your own individual. Don't be afraid to let your creative side out.

Accept the struggles in life. It's not your job to control what happens next. Put it in God's hands, and He'll take care of the rest.

POEMS

Poem written for Michelle on her thirteenth birthday and published in "The Colors of Life," The International Library of Poetry:

Teenage Bundle of Joy

Waiting so anxiously for this bundle of joy

to find out on Easter Sunday, that it was not a boy;

How perfect she was just looking at me

and realized she was as beautiful as could be;

She became our little precious moment

With her big beautiful blues

And watching her grow up so fast, while not having a clue;

The shoes, the hair, and the clothes have to match

In hopes of attracting that one special catch;

As boys will come and go you'll see

That Daddy's girl you'll always be;

Friendship and memories, more laughter than tears

while growing and learning from all of your fears;

Becoming a teenager came way too fast

look toward the future and learn from your past;

Continue your passions and whatever it seems

it's just the beginning of your hopes and dreams.

Poem I wrote to my mom before she passed away:

My Mother-My Best Friend

Celebrate her life without any fear

Remember the laughter not all the tears

A woman so strong and full of life

Is how she became a wonderful

Friend, Mother, Grandmother and Wife

Many lessons she taught

Whether you were family or not

"Money can't buy what I have each day

The love of our family

In an unconditional way"

Miles never separated her Family or Friends

Those memories will be cherished

In our hearts to the end!

We loved you yesterday and today even more

We'll love you tomorrow and forevermore.

December 2007

MY JOURNEY NOT MY DESTINATION

It has been quite the journey so far. And, I look forward to the doors God will open and close to serve His purpose. Was it a take-away journey for you? I pray God gave you hope along my journey; to know He is always there, loves you unconditionally and created you to be the best "YOU."

For me, I would not change one part of my journey. God gave me incredible strength when I wanted to give up, and He created the beautiful woman I am today. It has taken all this time, thus far, to say that. I have hope and believe I can get through anything when I put my life in God's hands.

I learned that everything we do can make a difference, whether we know it at the time, later in life, or be an unknown gift to another. Our simple words and actions can change a life. Our own experiences, or ones we share, can create a lasting spark for someone's future.

Sometimes choices do not make sense to some, but for the one going through it, it does makes sense. That is why it is so important not to judge a book by its cover or judge the chapter you walked into. It took until I became an adult, to find out why my mom left that day when I was in middle school. The details were never important or what defined her. She made a choice she needed to make at the time and her selflessness touched many lives along her journey.

Years later, I not only forgave the family member who abused me but had a yearning to drive past that once painful place, hoping to find an angel sitting by the oak tree. But, to my surprise, the apartment building was gone. A fire destroyed the building and it was torn down, never to be built again. It was as though God lead me to the place I once felt anger, to find peace in my heart from forgiveness, so I could continue to move forward serving Him.

Throughout the Bible, Jesus uses parables to teach us, stories to help us understand and be connected to the lesson. Our own stories are messages from our messes. Our stories are our parables to share with others, giving them hope.

God had a plan and purpose for my premature little boy, who is now twenty-six years old, and a Staff Sergeant in the United States Air Force. Nik's love for airplanes drew his interest in joining the Air Force, and he is currently an Armament Systems Technician. From holding a metal toy jet in his hand as a child, to working on jets as an adult. Every experience is a life changing experience.

God gave my mom many gifts and life lessons to share with many. My mom never had the opportunity to know that our "spa" and "skincare" experiences had such an impact on Michelle. Michelle had the desire to learn more about skincare and received scholarship funds to attend one of Aveda's Institute's "The Institute of Beauty and Wellness," in Milwaukee, Wisconsin. Michelle passed her state boards and became a licensed esthetician, which opened many doors and experiences that helped her as an Area Manager of a MedSpa in Colorado.

I have met so many angels along my journey. Ones who have helped me and others who I have helped; some are still in my life while others just passed through. There are no coincidences with God. He guided me through some tough times, even when I was ready to give up; He helped me survive them all because I trusted Him and put my life in His hands.

At times, we are only there (wherever "there" is) when needed. Like teachers, we are there to help students during the school day; mentors are there when mentee's need them; friends are there for each other in crises; but God never leaves us, even when we put Him aside when our life seems to be going well and we don't think we "need" Him.

What will the perception of your life's journey be like? If a change or move is part of your journey, will you be afraid of the unknown, or embrace what God has planned for you? It may be the time you meet a new lifelong friend, acquire the job you never imagined was possible, or understand why an angel came into your life at that time. God has already mapped out your life from the day you were born; enjoy the journey, and all the angels and life experiences along the way. When we put our life in God's hands, whether or not we know the "why," we can get through the "how" and understand our purpose. Life has meaning.

God gives us free will. When life feels like our faith is being tested, worries, concerns, and struggles are too great, put it all in God's hands, you'll no longer feel like Job, as God has a plan for you. Believe there is always HOPE.

You will decide on a matter, and it will be established for you, and light will shine on your ways. Job 22:28 NRSVCE

My broken journey gave me wonderful experiences. I have lived in different states, have met many people, and have had a variety of job opportunities. It led me to Craig amd a wonderful blended family, and brought me full circle—back to Wisconsin, which gave me more time to spend with my mother and Michelle and Nik more time with their grandparents.

I have had more amazing volunteer opportunities, I am a small business owner, and I am a published author. There were so many more experiences in that time, and I know there are many more yet to come.

God has not only blessed my life, turned all my trials to triumph, messes to messages, and brokenness to breakthrough, but has a great sense of humor. He brings light to every darkness. The number seven was more significant than I ever imagined. Craig and I were married after seven years of dating, and this year, 2019, we celebrate our 7th wedding anniversary!

I never gave up hope. I put my life in God's hands and will continue along, my once broken journey, towards His beautiful destination. My hope is for YOU, too, to never give up!

Hope is in the heart of the believer.

For everyone who asks receives, and everyone who searches finds, and for everyone who knocks, the door will be opened.
Matthew 7:8 NIV

Nik gives the BEST Hugs!

Our Family

Michelle and her
husband, Chris, at
their wedding

The Kids' First Christmas as a Family

Suprise College visit with the kids

Brotherly Love!

Their sister all grown up and married!
Nik, Michelle, Mitchell, and Austin

It's a tradition, when the kids are together,
we find a tree and take an updated picture.

2011

2015

Our Wedding Day

With Father John,
who co-officiated our Wedding

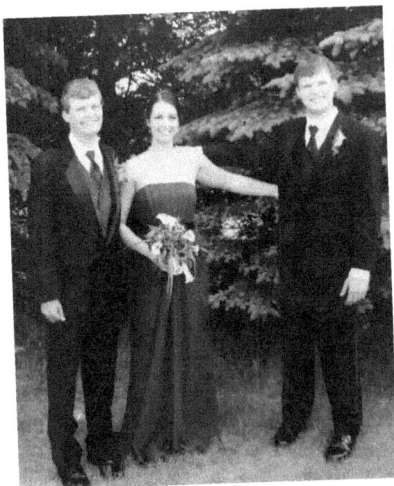

Austin, Michelle, and Mitchell
stood up in our wedding. Nik
was deployed to South Korea.

Our furry baby, Tucker

At the Markham Vineyard in CA

ACKNOWLEDGMENTS

First and foremost, I thank God for the opportunity to write this book, make dreams come true and for all the people He put in my life along this journey, including you, the Reader.

I will forever be grateful for my husband Craig, who tells me every day how beautiful I am; for the countless memories of going places I only dreamed of; and looking forward to the next 44 years with you, before all bets are off; thank you for encouraging me to fulfill my writing dreams; help me stay focused and giving me gentle reminders to put life in God's hands when I was discouraged; and for being supportive and understanding when I needed silence and couldn't always go on the weekend trips up north.

I am extremely thankful for my beautiful and resilient children Michelle and Nik; for your constant love, support, strength and encouragement when I needed it the most; and for the gift and honor of being your momma and sharing God's love, knowledge and wisdom with you to carry on.

A heartfelt thank you to Mitchell and Austin for loving me and allowing me to be the best step-mom I can. I am very proud of you two and all you have accomplished.

A special thanks to Michelle and Chris for giving me the best gift ever, my grandson Cole in 2019, and, like my mom and I, no amount of distance will ever separate us.

Saying "thank you" doesn't seem enough, John Kettelberger. Distance never separated your love, support and endless encouragement. I will be eternally grateful for everything, especially for writing such a special Foreword in "In God's Hands."

A special thank you to Victoria Kroonblawd for being a God-given gift in my life; a friend, mentee, prayer warrior, adopted daughter and for introducing me to Gillian. May God continue to bless you, Cory and your precious baby.

I could not have turned God's visions into His masterpieces without the incredible gifted Graphic Designer Gillian Miller. Thank you…thank you…thank you, Gillian, for sharing your God-given talents, the beautiful book design, and for the wonderful friendship God has blessed us with.

Thank you, Penny Fritsch, for sharing your God-given gift of photography and artist eye to capture just the right natural picture for the cover.

A big thank you to Marla McKenna, my friend and editor, who encourages me to keep writing and share my story to help others, giving them hope along their journey.

Thank you to Mike Nicloy, an amazing publisher and friend. I can't thank you enough for making it so comfortable to work with you. You are a gift to many!

I am eternally grateful for each and every one of my friends and family members who have stood by my side, never judged, and loved me unconditionally as the real, raw and authentic "Me" God created. If I were to thank everyone individually who has touched my life and made a difference in it, that would be a book in itself. So, thank you, from the bottom of my heart, for coming into my life for whatever reason or purpose that only God may know, as each person and experience has made me who I am today.

I love and appreciate you all!

ABOUT the AUTHOR

Mary Markham is the founder of Inspirational Visions LLC (www.inspirationalvisionsllc.com), an author, mentor, and coordinator for Family Promise of Waukesha County, a non-profit organization helping homeless families with children, and she is the contributing author of the bestselling book, *The Miracle Effect.*

Mary enjoys sharing her God-inspired simple messages; "Let Go Let God," "I AM," and, "Broken Not Shattered," as well as spending time with her family and friends, traveling, biking, and gardening.

Mary and her husband, Craig, reside in Wisconsin, and between them they have four independent and successful children.

www.ingramcontent.com/pod-product-compliance
Lightning Source LLC
LaVergne TN
LVHW051232080426
835513LV00016B/1550